THE ART OF
FALLING IN LOVE
WITH YOUR
TIME ON EARTH

THE ART OF FALLING IN LOVE WITH YOUR TIME ON EARTH

Mannie Billig

LUTHERS
New Smyrna Beach
FLORIDA

Published by
LUTHERS
1009 North Dixie Freeway
New Smyrna Beach, FL 32168-6221
www.lutherspublishing.com

LIBRARY OF CONGRESS
CATALOGING-IN-PUBLICATION DATA
Billig, Mannie, 1942–
The art of falling in love
with your time on earth / Mannie Billig.
p.   cm.
ISBN: 1-877633-74-7 (pbk.)
1. Spiritual life. I. Title.
BL624.B495 2004
204'.4—dc22
2004061615

DEDICATION

This book is dedicated to my mother, Connie Billig, whose dedication to her two boys was unquestioned. Even though she had many difficulties in her life, she never gave up. She passed away in 1985, and I love and miss her very much.

The loving support and contributions of my wife, Judy Billig, are woven through the pages of this book. Judy's dedication and hard work are deeply appreciated.

FOREWORD

The purpose of this book is for your highest and best good. Like a flower opening to the sun, receive it with an open heart and open mind. This message is sent with unconditional love. Take from it what you will.

As we go through life, we begin to understand the purpose of our journey. Each experience is an opportunity to grow and expand our soul. This book's purpose is to help us understand how to improve the quality of our life.

We can create an environment within our own mind that will allow us to understand our own unique spirituality. By realizing our own spirituality, we can come into a true experience of the presence of God.

I believe that you only see God's presence in another person to the extent that you see God's presence within yourself. This is the thread that connects us all.

Knowing where to start is the key. We can read a thousand books and go to dozens of seminars and not find what we are looking for. You can devote your life to traveling the world in search of yourself and never realize that wherever you go, you have to take yourself with you.

The journey is within your soul and your heart as you realize that you are here to find the purpose to your life. Inner peace and happiness aren't something that someone else can give you; they are something that you give yourself. When we become more loving and kinder human beings, we will have experiences that will make us think that the world has changed. However, the world hasn't changed. Our perception of the world has changed. When our perception of the world changes, how we feel about life will change.

Once we have the desire to improve our quality of life, then we have the choice to seek the knowledge to open the door to our life's purpose. Knock and the door shall be opened, if you so desire.

This book is a guide to help you become the wise master of your soul's development. Drawing from my own life experiences, I write about how difficult situations in our life can turn out to be blessings.

The exercises included in this book are designed to aid in understanding the events of your life and how these events work to develop your soul.

This book has two basic parts. I describe the events that created the lessons in my life in part one. This includes how life lessons were brought to me and the knowledge and wisdom that I gained from each experience. Sometimes I knew what the purpose of each event was almost from the minute that it happened. Other times it took years to realize what was happening and the purpose of the lesson I was learning.

In the second part of the book, I describe the benefits of these life lessons by putting them together in an organized fashion. I offer the reader an opportunity to consider how following the suggestions made in part two of the book would affect their own life. This isn't something you have to, it is something you get to do.

TABLE OF CONTENTS

Chapter 1
THE AWAKENING

In 1968, I was sitting in a theater watching the original version of the movie, "Planet of the Apes." Charlton Heston had the starring role in this movie about a group of astronauts who crash land on a planet. The planet is strange to them, and they have no idea where they are.

One of the most shocking scenes in the movie occurs near the end of the film. Charlton Heston's character and his companions approach an area of land that is barren and lifeless.

In the distance they can see a large object jutting out of the sand. Charlton Heston's character uses his binoculars to see what the object is. As the object comes into focus he mutters in disbelief, "What the hell happened?"

The object on the horizon turned out to be the Statue of Liberty laying on the ground and broken into several pieces. Heston's character then realized that he was not on some strange, foreign planet. He was on Earth, and civilization as he had known it had vanished.

At that very moment, my entire life flashed before my eyes. I saw myself lying on my deathbed, and it was the last day of my life.

Questions began rolling through my mind. What happened? How come I hadn't lived the life that I wanted?

Why did I just drift along in the river of life and never take control? Why had I made the choices that I made, just going along with the crowd and not following my dreams?

Why had I lost my smile and my zest for life? Why had I been so serious and not enjoyed every day of my life? I didn't have any idea what the real purpose of my life was meant to be.

What did I want out of my life? Why was I here? Was it to see how much money I could make in a lifetime? Does the person with the most material goods win? What is it that they win? Doesn't the way we live our lives make any difference?

When I looked back from my deathbed, I was no longer willing to just drift in the river of life without any direction.

From that day on, I completely changed the way I looked at life. I was asking myself some very tough questions. Did my mother know how much I loved her? Why was I here on this Earth? Why was I so tough on everyone including myself? How come I hadn't found happiness? What had my life meant to me?

My life had to have more meaning than just how much money I could make, or how many toys I could accumulate. I decided that I would start a journey to find my life's purpose.

That vision helped me change my life for the better. I had a chance to change my priorities in life. It was like being born again and being able to start over with a new outlook on life. How happy I was to have this opportunity!

When I realized what had happened, tears came to my eyes. I had discovered what was meant by the expression about people who look but don't see, people who listen but don't hear, and people who touch but don't feel. I had awakened from my despair.

I decided that I would become the master of my life, and I would take my soul's development seriously. I didn't have to live my life in a rut. I realized that I had the power to change my entire outlook on life.

SETTING PRIORITIES IN MY LIFE

After I had the vision of seeing myself lying on my deathbed, my idea of what was really important in life changed. Before the vision, I had blind ambition, just going along in the river of life without much thought other than just trying to succeed.

I thought that success was measured by how much money I made and what kind of car I drove. An impressive job title was also very important to me as it meant that I had made it. But it never seemed enough. I wanted to be a store manager, and once I was a small store manager, I wanted a bigger store. Once I had a bigger store, I wanted the biggest store in the chain.

I had several experiences that made me realize that I wasn't in control of my life. As an example, the phone would ring. I was told several times, eleven times to be exact, that I was being transferred to a city several hundred miles away. I usually had to be there in a couple of days. At first it was exciting because I enjoyed the new challenge of working with different people and circumstances. But after I had the vision of seeing myself on my deathbed, I realized that I had forgotten about my dream to own my own business. This brought my original intention back into focus.

What I really wanted was to have control of my life by owning my own business. If I could run a large store for a major corporation, why couldn't I run a small one for myself? If it really was the last day of my life, what would I think about the fact that I never had the courage to go for my dream of owning my own business?

When I would imagine that it was my last day to live, I didn't feel right about the fact that I hadn't even tried to make my dream of owning my own store come true. I could accept it if I had tried to have my own business and it wasn't successful. But if I didn't even try to achieve my dream, I felt it would be something I would always regret.

So I started a plan to make my dream a reality. I used the vision of being on my deathbed to help me decide to be my own boss.

What did I want out of life? As I asked myself that question, I realized that my priorities had changed. Every second of my life was much more important to me. How would I spend my time on Earth was just as important as what I accomplished. I would no longer give my very life, my time on Earth, to things I didn't truly enjoy.

I started to make a life plan to point me in the direction I wanted to go. For example, I knew that I didn't like working at night or on Sundays, so I wouldn't do anything that would require me to work nights or Sundays. I had always wanted to have my own business. It was important for me to take control of my life. I could start a business, but it had to be one that fit into my life plan instead of me fitting my life plan into the business.

I can remember ordering a handbook of every franchise business available in the United States. I highlighted the businesses I was interested in and sent a form letter to each one. In a short time, I started to get their literature in the mail. As I would read each one, if it didn't fit into my life plan, I would discard it. If I wanted an 8 a.m. to 5 p.m. business, I wouldn't consider anything that didn't fit. I didn't want to get up at 3 a.m. to make doughnuts, and I didn't want to be closing a bar at 2 a.m.

I narrowed my choice down to two different businesses. They both fit into my life plan. The reason I chose one over the other was that the franchise opportunity for my first choice wasn't available in the part of the country that I wanted to live in. As I thought about my decision not to go with my first choice, I exercised my right to decide where I wanted to live.

I chose the tool rental business in Central Florida. Once I had picked the business and the area of country I wanted to live, there was still plenty to do. I had to arrange a complete physical examination to make sure I didn't have any life threatening illness because by quitting my corporate job, I would be losing my health benefits.

Next I wrote a business plan so I could obtain financing for my business venture. My business plan included a profit and loss budget and a summary as to the rational for the business venture. Once I had decided what general area I wanted to live in, then I could find a location for the business. I looked at several locations and chose one that I could have a lease option on to purchase the property after the business was established.

Then I submitted my business plan to a bank for review and approval. It took about three months before I got it approved. In the meantime, I went ahead and scheduled the medical examination that I wanted.

DOCTOR'S OFFICE VISIT

In the fall of 1983 I was living in Bloomington, Illinois. As part of my plan to take control of my life, I decided that before I left my corporate job and pursued my dream of owning my own business, I would be very thorough and get the best medical checkup available. I wanted to make sure that I didn't have any major health problems.

During my doctor's visit, I told the doctor about my vision of seeing the last day of my life and how I was going for my dream of opening my own business. I told him that the reason I wanted a complete physical was that I didn't want leave a corporate job with full benefits and then discover I had cancer or some other life threatening medical condition. I would continue to carry health insurance when I quit. But I didn't want to be stuck with pre-existing conditions that my new insurance company wouldn't cover. The doctor said he understood and gave the thorough examine that I requested.

Everything checked out fine. As the doctor was going over my results with me, he was very interested in the vision that I had about lying on my deathbed thinking back over my life. It was of some interest to him because it started him thinking about his own life.

He started to tell me his thoughts about how he would feel on the last day of his life. He revealed to me that he didn't really want to be a doctor. He said he was forced into it because he didn't want to be drafted into the

Vietnam war. At that time, if he stayed in school, he received a deferment from the draft. So he stayed in school and became a doctor.

He did not enjoy being a doctor because of the pressures and responsibility involved. He was tied down to his office and didn't have the freedom that he desired. The amount of responsibility he had to deal with as a doctor had not occurred to him when he chose to go to medical school. The life of a doctor was much different than he had thought it would be. It wasn't the leisurely life of country clubs and playing golf that he had envisioned.

He said it was difficult to even get a decent night's sleep because the phone would ring most nights with some type of emergency. After talking with his patients all day, he would go home stressed out and find it hard to go to sleep even on the nights the phone didn't ring. The next day the cycle would be repeated.

This type of lifestyle was stressing him out physically, mentally and emotionally. I suggested that he should consider changing his approach to his job or consider changing to some other line of work. He said that he would think about it, but he was concerned what his wife, parents and the community would think if he decided to stop being a doctor. Although he understood the effects of all the pressures on him and how it would affect his overall health and well being, he was hesitant to make any changes.

I told him about a man I knew who had earned a doctorate in electrical engineering. This man was very good at his job, but he really didn't enjoy it. The fact that his job took him to a big city also made him sad. He had grown up on a farm and had enjoyed living in the country.

Even though it involved hard, physical labor, he had enjoyed growing up on a farm. When he became an engineer, he moved to a large city, married and had children. He didn't like the city environment. He believed the city was a rough place for his children. After much thought and prayer, he quit his job as an electrical engineer and bought a farm in central Pennsylvania.

He said these moves completely changed his life because he was back to doing what he loved to do. His children loved the farm, and it brought his family closer together. There was something about being able to touch the earth and watch things grow that he missed when he was an electrical engineer. He wasn't a big shot on the farm, but he found the peace and tranquility that he had longed for.

The doctor thanked me for taking the time and interest in sharing my vision and stories with him. He said that he understood that he could try to do his work with a change of attitude and enjoy it, or he could consider doing something else. I moved away from that part of the country, so I never did find out how he came to peace with his life. Sometimes I think of him, and I hope he had the courage to adjust his life in such a way that he enjoyed every minute of it.

My complete medical physical revealed that I was healthy. Therefore, I continued with my plan to move to Florida and open my own business. My business loan was approved, and my dream of having my own business was becoming a reality.

After one and a half years of planning, I gave my resignation notice to the regional personnel manager. My employer did not want me to resign. I was told that they could pay me more money, and that I would have a good future with the corporation if I stayed. I thanked the personnel manager. I explained my vision to him, and said I couldn't enjoy my life if I died without going for my dreams. I told him that if I went for my dream and it wasn't a success, I would consider coming back as he had asked me to do. I was to the point that I had to open my own business so that I could live with myself, even if I did not succeed.

After the personnel manager knew I was leaving and he couldn't talk me out of it, he said that he wished he could go with me. The day I left that corporation was one of the happiest days of my life. I was free and felt like a heavy burden had been lifted off my shoulders. I went from making a good salary to having no salary, but

I was filled with excitement and joy. That was the last day I ever wore a suit to work.

Having the courage to put my dream into action was one of the best decisions I have ever made. It started me toward the goal of finding my life's purpose. A big part of the journey was stepping out of my comfort zone and finding out the reason I had the dream in the first place. It was part of my life's journey to trust myself and my feelings of what is important in life to me.

Some people thought I was crazy to give up such a good job since I had worked my way up the corporate ladder. When I worked for the retail corporation, they kept me so busy running a department store that there wasn't much time for me to think about what I really wanted, about my purpose in life and how my journey would unfold.

I thanked them for all the training and opportunity that they gave me. I realized that if I could run a store doing millions of dollars for them, I could certainly run a small store for myself. Part of my plan was to make enough money to live on, but not to become obsessed with money. All I needed was the basics of life. What I was seeking was the opportunity to have the time to start the true journey to find my life's purpose.

I went from having a job to really looking forward to each moment of my day. Life had become very exciting to me. I had found the joy and zest for life that I had somehow lost in the corporate world. I have been in business for over twenty years and have never regretted my decision to follow my dream to start my own business.

Chapter 2
STARTING TO FALL IN LOVE
WITH MY LIFE

I opened my business in June 1984 in Casselberry, Florida. One of the biggest advantages of owning my own business was the amount of freedom it has given me to relax and think about my life. One of the best decisions I ever made was to take meditation classes. I started meditation classes in the early 1990s. I was with a group of people who were searching for inner peace and happiness.

At first, I found it hard to completely relax my mind and connect with the bliss that was there for me. I really enjoyed being with the other members of the class and looked forward to the class each week. We would sit in a circle and just relax our minds and allow the stress of the day to just melt away. We would meditate for ten to fifteen minutes. Then we would discuss whatever feelings we had, and how we each looked at different problems that some in the group wanted to discuss. It seemed to help each person to be in a support group that didn't judge them. Class members would listen and give suggestions if anyone asked for suggestions.

After a few classes, I would start to talk during the meditation. The teacher encouraged us to allow whatever was going to happen to unfold. In other words, we started to get in touch with the energy that is there for us. Sometimes I could feel the energy, and it would move my body. It was almost like listening to a love song and just getting in touch with the beauty of the song. When you are in touch with the beauty of a song, you feel like you are floating on a cloud or falling in love. The only difference is that you just start to fall in love with life. It is a wonderful feeling, and I felt comfortable allowing whatever was going to happen to just happen.

When I started to talk during our meditations, some of the most wonderful words of encouragement would come out of me. I really didn't understand what the origin of the words was. I wasn't thinking about what to say, but it was like the love that I had in my heart was just coming out of me.

After attending the meditation classes for about six months, I had the opportunity to go to a weekend seminar taught by a teacher from the Far East. Most of the group from the meditation class went, and there were a large number of other people in attendance. It was a three-day seminar, and I had no idea what to expect. But I knew that I wanted to participate in this seminar.

When the seminar started, the teacher asked us to meditate. After a short meditation, he would ask some of the participants questions as he moved around the room. He began talking to the man next to me. This man was a doctor. The teacher asked him some questions. Then the teacher made some statements to the doctor. The first statement he made to the doctor was, "You have a lot of problems in your life, don't you?" The doctor replied, "Yes, I do." The teacher then said, "See the man next to you, he has had many problems in his life, but he has been able to overcome them." The teacher was talking about me.

Then the teacher asked the doctor, "When the was the last time you saw your brother?" The doctor said, "I have two brothers. Which one are you talking about?" The teacher said, "The tall one." The doctor said, "I haven't been in touch with him for over ten years." The teacher asked him why he hadn't been in touch with his brother. The doctor replied, "My brother is an alcoholic and pretty much the black sheep of the family." The teacher told him, "He is your brother and he needs you."

As the doctor started to understand what the teacher said, tears started to come down his face. He realized his brother needed his help. That night the doctor with his new outlook on life called his brother. They talked for quite a while and renewed their relationship. The next day at class, the doctor said they were going to get together and be as brothers should be. This is an example of how we are brought spiritual lessons by other people in our lives.

At that moment, I thought about my relationship with my mother and my dad. It may have been one of the first times I realized that they didn't have easy lives. I also realized that part of my life's journey was to experience the need for love in my life. At that point, it was obvious to me that they had participated in the development of my soul. Having them as parents gave me unique experiences that I may not have understood while I was going through them.

That evening, I thought about the doctor's relationship with his brother, and how it was an opportunity to apply what I had learned from that to my own life. If there are outcasts or black sheep in our family or other relationships, aren't we all in life's school? Aren't the lessons we go through sometimes painful, but necessary? If we can open our minds and hearts, we can look at the experiences in a different way.

When I decided to apply the doctor's experiences to my own life, I started to have a better understanding of the reason I had the life experiences that I had with my parents. That evening I thought back about the relationship that I had with my father and my mother. When I was seven years old, my father left our family, and we never heard from him. We didn't get any support or communications from him. It really bothered me a lot because I didn't know what we had done to make him leave. I adjusted to the lifestyle, but something really

11

made me wonder why this was happening to me.

When I would go to visit one of my schoolmates at their house, their parents would ask me where my dad was employed. I never could feel comfortable telling them that my dad had left us, and I had no idea where he was living. It always gave me a knot in the pit of my stomach and upset me, but I would tell them that my dad had left, and I had no idea where he worked or lived. They would be nice about it, but it didn't help my feelings. One day in my early twenties an older co-worker asked me where my dad worked. I shared my feelings with him about what had happened in my life and how it made me feel.

He told me that he was carrying a burden of sadness because of what had happened in his life with his father. He got into an argument with his father, and they didn't speak to each other for ten years. He got a call one day telling him that his father had passed away. He really felt guilty that he hadn't tried to patch things up with his dad. He couldn't even remember what the argument was about. He said that he would give everything he had in the world just to see his father for one minute, so he could tell him how sorry he was and how much he loved him. He told me that if I ever got the chance to meet my dad that I should go for it because of what had happened to him.

I understood what he was talking about. But I must admit that I never thought that I would have to confront that situation. Life went on and I never found out about my dad until I was thirty years old. One day I got a phone call from my grandmother, his mother, telling me that doctors had found cancer in my dad. The doctors gave him six months to live. She wanted to know if I could forgive him for what he had done, and would I go see him. She said that she thought it would help him, but she understood the decision was mine to make.

I recalled what my friend had told me about his dad dying before they could speak to each other. They had never been able to tell each other how much they loved one other, and how sorry they were about the stupid argument. I had a choice to make. I could go the rest of my life never knowing my dad, or I could chose to forgive him and know him from the moment we met until one of us passed on. I chose to go and meet him and see what had happened with our relationship.

My grandmother and my dad met me at the airport, and we spent a week getting to get reacquainted. We went camping up in the Rocky Mountains and had some time to get to know one another. I enjoyed the week that I spent with him, and he was very sad the day he took me back to the airport. He said that he had thought about me and my brother every day of his life. He was sorry that things had worked out the way the way that they did. He wanted to make sure that I knew how much he loved me and how much he appreciated my visit.

As we were driving to the airport, he told me several things that really helped me understand. He said that he had realized at that moment he wasn't supposed to be there to raise me. If he would have been there, he would have messed me up. He was an alcoholic, and he didn't like himself very much. At that very moment I realized that he was right. If he would have been there, it would have been a much more difficult life for me. At the age of thirty I realized that I had a wonderful childhood, but I just didn't know it while I was growing up.

As I was sitting on the airplane, I started to think about my childhood. How lucky I was to have a mother who loved me and did her best to provide for me while I was growing up. I also thought about what my dad had told me about his life. He was two when his dad had died, and he was put into an orphanage. He got into some trouble and was put into a reformatory school.

He had met my mother at the age of sixteen and married her. They had a daughter named Marlene, who was killed when she was two years old. She ran out into the street and was run over by a car. He was in the service when she died.

Is it any wonder that he couldn't cope and stared to drink? How could I judge my dad when I didn't know what had happened in his life? How can we judge anyone without walking a mile in their shoes?

My relationship with my dad continued for another thirty years until he passed away. He became one of my best friends and helped me understand that the experiences in my life had helped me learn my life's lessons.

A song by Mike and the Mechanics called "In the Living Years" explains how I feel about my mother. I really didn't understand the sacrifices that my mother had made for my brother and me while we were growing up. After my father left, I recall being on a street corner with my mother as she was talking to one of her girl friends. She told my mother that she was moving to California and asked my mother to come with her. She said my mother could put my brother and me in an orphanage. My mom thought about it for a couple of seconds and made a commitment that she would dedicate the rest of her life to. Mom said that she wanted to raise her two boys and wouldn't be moving to California.

When my dad left, times were very difficult for my family. I can remember walking with my mom to the railroad tracks to pick up coal that had fallen off the train cars. She taught me that you could get more coal where there were curves in the tracks because the coal would fall off more easily when the train was going around a bend. We needed that coal to keep us warm because it was very cold in Greenville, Pennsylvania in the winter, and we had very little money.

The home we rented consisted of three rooms, plus a bathroom. There was only one bedroom. I slept on a couch in the living room. I never had my own bed until I joined the Army in July 1960.

Food was very scarce, and we lived on welfare until my mother was able to get a job. She landed a job in a factory as a welder to support us. She would come home so tired that she would make our supper and pass out on the couch. Then the next morning she would get up at 5 a.m. and go to work again.

The job was draining the very life out of her day by day, but she never gave up or quit. I can't say that I understood my mother or the sacrifices she made while

14

I was growing up. We didn't know how to communicate with each other because she was a very outspoken person, and I was embarrassed to be in public with her. She was angry with the way her life had worked out, but she never gave up.

As I grew up, I was also angry because I didn't have what other kids had. For example, we didn't have a car and when we went for groceries, we had to walk home with everything we bought. It didn't matter if it was raining or if it was twenty below zero, we walked everywhere we went. The high school was about three miles away, and I had to walk since there wasn't bus service provided to that part of town. It wasn't any fun going to school with wet clothes if it was raining. I thought that my mother didn't like me very much when I was growing up. I didn't understand why I didn't get much guidance from her.

When I was sixteen, she bought a car for me. She didn't drive, so she was trying her best to help me. I joined the Army after I graduated from high school and never looked back or appreciated the sacrifices that my mom had made for me. Life went on for me as I tried to improve my life, and I never really thought about all that my mom had done for me. I knew that I wanted to help mom, but I would do it later. One day I got a call from my brother saying that mom had died. I was stunned to say the least. I really felt bad because I had never realized that at some point life ends. The intentions I had never materialized into actions for mom.

At the funeral my cousin made a comment to me that really floored me. She said how much she had respected my mother and us kids because we were a family. The fact that my mother cared enough about my brother and me to stay and raise us really impressed her. Her mother left her with our grandmother to raise and never went back to get her or her two brothers. At that moment, I realized that I had the best mom in the whole world because she put us kids before herself. She did her best and what more could anyone ask.

After the funeral I went to visit one of my mom's best

friends. She had not been able to attend the funeral because she had a stroke and was very ill. She explained how when I was still in diapers that my sister and I were on the porch. The baby sitter took me into the house to change my diaper. My sister walked off the porch and into the street and was killed by a car. This devastated my mom. She loved my sister so much, and her death affected my mom so deeply that it changed her. She never wanted to experience such a great loss in her life again, so she withdrew from me emotionally. She was heartbroken and sad for the rest of her life.

I wish that I could have known the circumstances of mom's life. It would have helped me understand the reasons she made the decisions that she did. This experience was part of my awakening to make me a more understanding, loving human being. As the song "In the Living Years" goes, "Every generation blames the one before, I just wish I would have said the things I have to say in the living years." Mom, I love and appreciate you more than you ever knew. I only hope that I can be half as good a person as you were a mother.

I have to admit that I get emotional when I think of the sacrifices that my parents made for me. Although I hadn't evolved to the extent I wanted at the time of my mom's passing, her unexpected passing helped awaken me to how precious every moment of our life is. Good intentions are one thing, but unless we put them into action, we can miss a lot in our lives.

The teacher from the Far East stressed how important meditating each day was in helping us in our connection to God. I had enjoyed my experience, and I attended a couple more of his seminars. At the last seminar, he came to me during one of the meditations and asked me why I was still attending his seminars. He said it was time for me to move on and teach to others the lessons that I had learned.

Chapter 3
WHEN THE STUDENT IS READY, THE TEACHER WILL APPEAR

There have been many teachers who have come into my life. Sometimes I realized that they were my teacher, and sometimes I didn't. A mentor that you like and respect is someone that is easier to identify as you listen to what they have to say and watch how they handle different situations.

I had the opportunity to meet such a man. His name was Dr. Hermia Nobileo, Ph.D. D.D. I met him in Jacksonville, Florida at a time when I was having employee problems at my corporate job. I was asked by one of my employees if I would like to meet a man from India who could help me with my problems. I decided to meet with him based on the glowing report that Dr. Nobileo received from that employee.

I was told that Dr. Nobileo didn't charge anything. He had a small church on the north side of Jacksonville that helped people in need. This occurred back in early 1977, after I had been assigned to one of the twenty worst profit and problem department stores in a chain of around 400 stores. The first day I arrived at the store, I met the district manager at 7:00 a.m. to do an audit review of the store's performance. Because of poor supervision and leadership, the previous manager had been demoted along with most of his staff. About half of the store's management was replaced just before I received the assignment to go there.

The name of the store was Jacksonville Gateway. The first words out of the district manager's mouth were, "If there is a Gateway store in heaven, I don't want to go to heaven." That was the district manager's way of telling me how bad the conditions were at this store. I knew he was right because I had had to sit in an audit review of the store's problems for eleven hours and listen to how poorly the store had been run. To my knowledge, no store manager had ever been promoted out of this store. In fact, most managers from the store had ended their careers with the corporation after being assigned there.

Many of the managers felt that the store had a curse on it. Some managers felt that the store was occupied by evil spirits. It was located on the north side of Jacksonville in a very rough part of town. One of the employees told me that in most stores, workers look to see if someone stole a watch or piece of jewelry out of a display case. The employee explained that at this particular store you would check to see if someone stole the display case and all the jewelry in it.

This store had such a bad reputation within the company that insiders would often joke about how incredibly bad the conditions were at that location. Before long, I realized that I was in a very tough situation, and it would take all of my efforts to straighten out the store.

Some of the employees wouldn't come to work on time, had poor attitudes and were basically just giving up. They thought the store was hopeless. If you were an employee from the Gateway store, somehow you were tarnished, and most of the other stores and district staff thought that you were stupid.

I knew that I could straighten out the store if I was given the support and guidance to do the job. Having never dealt with a store that had a perceived curse on it, I agreed to meet with Dr. Nobileo.

When I called Dr. Nobileo, he invited me to meet with

him at his home. When I arrived at his home, I was surprised to see that he was a frail old man. He welcomed me into his home to sit and talk for a while. As we spoke, he would close his eyes and draw circles on a tablet. Then he asked me if my deceased grandfather was blind in one eye.

I wondered how he would know that since I barely remembered that fact about my grandfather. Dr. Nobileo said my deceased grandfather was looking at him in his mind's eye, and he was favoring one side as if he had lost sight in the other eye. These remarks shocked me because I had never been exposed to someone with this kind of psychic ability. Dr. Nobileo told me several things that got my attention that day.

As we talked, I felt he was someone that I wanted to get to know better. I could see the wisdom in his words and manner. Before I left that day, he said the person who had recommended that I meet with him had indicated I had a lot of problems at work. After meeting me, Dr. Nobileo said I was fine, but that I was in a very stressful environment. He recommended that I buy an ivy plant with green leaves and place it in my office at that store. He said the plant would absorb the stress from the job, and as a result of this, some of the leaves of the plant would turn brown and die. These dead leaves were to be removed from the plant and then placed on the dirt inside the plant container. The dead leaves would help to nourish the plant.

I thanked him for taking his time to talk to me. I must admit I was overwhelmed by what he told me about my life. I could see he was a very wise man, and I chose to listen to the suggestion he made to me. The next day Dr. Nobileo came to the store and brought me the type of plant he had recommended for my office. He explained the store was not cursed, but it was in a rough part of town. This was why the store had so many problems. He said if I worked hard that I would be fine, but it would not be easy.

I really appreciated his going out of his way to bring me the plant. I had planned to buy a plant, but hadn't gotten around to it. It was nice to find someone with his wisdom who practiced what he preached.

After a week or two, I noticed a few of the leaves dying on the ivy plant. I pulled the dead leaves off and put them on the dirt in the plant container as he had instructed. Believe it or not, I felt the plant did help me. I became more relaxed with my new position.

A few days later, I invited Dr. Nobileo to lunch because I really appreciated his efforts to help me. We went to a very busy restaurant. As we were pulling into the outer edge of the parking lot, I told him that I would drop him off at the entrance to the restaurant and then park the car. The parking lot was jammed, and I didn't think there would be any parking spaces available near the entrance. He looked at me and said there would be a parking space available for us right up front.

As we turned the corner to the front of the lot, a car was just pulling out of the first non-handicap parking space. I thought to myself, how did he know this would happen? Was it just luck, or did he know something that I didn't?

After having lunch with him several times, I realized it wasn't luck. It happened every time we went any-where. As we talked and I started to ask him questions as to why the parking spaces were always there, he laughed, "When you decide to follow the true meaning to your life's purpose, then the traffic light stays green for you. The parking spaces are there when you need them."

He talked about the ability to heal people with his mind. He had written a book titled, *A Complete Course in the Philosophy of Metaphysical Healing.* He was very knowledgeable about healing with our minds.

As I listened to him and absorbed all the knowledge that I could, my life started to change. Suddenly, I start-ed getting good parking spaces, and traffic lights seemed to stay green longer. The right people started to call, and I was on my way to realizing that I was a spir-itual being having a human experience, and there was more to learn in this lifetime. Every time I get a good parking spot, I think of Dr. Nobileo. He was a good friend and mentor.

Another example of my soul's development happened at the store. It was an experience I had with one of the employees. As a store manager, I tried to get to know all of my employees and learn their goals. One of the women in the fashion accessory department was a very hard worker and very dependable. She was an African-American. She was very deserving of a promotion to the department manager level.

I worked to get her a promotion to the position of catalog manager. She adapted to the job very well, and I was pleased with her performance. Although business was tough in this department at the time, I recommended to my supervisor, the district manager, that she receive a salary increase.

Per corporate policy, I couldn't tell her about my recommendation for the salary increase until it was approved. As things sometimes happen, my supervisor rejected the request because of the poor sales at that time. The fact that sales were poor was a valid reason for him to reject my request. When she asked me for a salary increase, I had to tell her that the company was not approving salary increases because of poor sales.

She knew that I thought she was doing a good job because I had told her so on several occasions. When she didn't receive a salary increase, she was very upset. I couldn't tell her that I recommended a raise, but my supervisor wouldn't approve her salary increase.

To make a long story short, she filed a discrimination suit against me. She found it hard to understand why I would tell her how pleased I was with her work, but not give her a larger paycheck. From her viewpoint, I could understand her feelings. But from my viewpoint, I was her biggest supporter.

I was caught between a rock and a hard place. When she filed the discrimination case, the regional staff became involved and thought she was a troublemaker. I told the regional staff that I didn't view her as a troublemaker even though she had filed a discrimination case against me. I still did what I could to help her.

The discrimination case was investigated and dismissed by the government. When that happened she decided to give two weeks notice and quit. I asked her to come to my office. I told her that I thought she was doing a good job, and I convinced her not to quit. The regional staff found out that she had given notice and became very upset with me because I had talked her out of resigning. They thought I was stupid for asking her to stay when she had caused so much trouble for me and the company.

I felt it was more important to do what was right than to let someone think I didn't appreciate their hard work. She eventually did get the salary increase that I had originally requested. We worked well together until I was transferred to another store. I heard after I left that she eventually left the company.

This experience was an example of how we get to do the right thing even though some circumstances are beyond our control. I view her as one of my teachers in a way because I was tested in my dealings with her. I stuck with the truth instead of going the easy route and agreeing with my supervisor. I feel she eventually understood her lesson in this experience because when I left the store, she knew I had had a high regard for her ability. She was a proud person, and I am a better man because I had the opportunity to share this experience with her.

If you knew the person that you were having the learning experience with was helping you develop your very soul, would you feel differently about them? Would you be grateful instead of being bitter and hateful? The truth is they could be like an actor in a play. Would we feel the same way if that was the case?

Many people can be teachers in our lives. They help us experience life's lessons. Sometimes we will recognize them as teachers, and sometimes we won't. If we can learn to be the observer in our very life, we can understand the benefit from that particular experience. The way we feel about the experience can help us move on to our next lesson, or the lesson may have to be repeated if we don't get the benefit of the lesson the first time.

The point I want to make about the lessons that I will experience in my life is that I want to experience what I am here to learn, but I would like to be able to move on to the next lesson without repeating many lessons.

When you start to look at a difficult experience as being helpful in your development and you embrace it, you can move through lessons more quickly. You may not understand the benefit of each lesson at the time you are going through them. In fact, it may be several years before you understand why things happened the way they did.

For example, one of the men I worked with hated his job and always complained about it. It was affecting his health, but he wouldn't quit his job. Then one day he was fired. The universe took him out of that job because he didn't listen to his feelings and quit on his own. Now he has a job working with children, and he loves it. I wonder how many kids he has helped in his new job. He is where he is supposed to be for now.

I'm sure it was an unpleasant experience getting fired, but it was necessary to move him on his life's path. When we know that the things that happen in our life are for our benefit even if we can't understand that at the time, we are more at peace in our life. It's like playing cards. You have to play the hand that you are dealt to the best of your ability. It's what you are here to learn. So we can choose to embrace life and its challenges, or we can struggle with them. It is our choice.

Chapter 4
LOOKING FOR
THE PURPOSE TO MY LIFE

WAKE UP CALL

One summer evening in the 1990s after finishing my evening meal, I felt a severe pain in my chest and back. The thought crossed my mind that if it was time for my life to end, I wasn't ready to go. However, the pain was so severe that I knew I wouldn't want to continue to live if I had to endure it on a daily basis.

I went to the emergency room and had an EKG and an examination by the emergency room doctor. Everything looked okay, but I was referred back to my doctor for further evaluation. He set me up for more tests. The tests revealed that I had gall stones, and my gall bladder would have to be removed. I was relieved that the cause of my pain and suffering had been diagnosed. We set up an appointment to have the gall bladder removed. At that time the idea of having my gall bladder removed didn't seem like a big deal.

I went to the hospital early one morning and prepared to have my operation. Everything seemed to be going okay, and I figured it would be over in a day. While I was waiting to be wheeled into the surgery room, a nurse came up to me. She said, "I hope everything goes okay for you today." She was just wishing me good luck, and I am sure she meant well. All of a sudden, I realized that sometimes everything doesn't go okay. I became quite concerned because the thought had never crossed my mind that everything might not be okay.

As I was lying there waiting for surgery, I thought about my life. I was glad that I had made the choices that I did in my life. I had opened my own business and was enjoying being my own boss. I felt in harmony with life and had a smile on my face.

During this time, I could hear footsteps coming down the hall from the operating room several times. When would they come for me? Eventually, they took me down the hall and put me into another waiting room. I guess this was the pre-op room where I would wait until I was the next one to go into surgery. Finally, they took me into the operating room and gave me a shot. I was out in no time flat and had no idea if I would ever see my friends and loved ones again.

The next thing I knew monitors were beeping, and I was in the post operating room recovering. The nurse said everything had gone okay, and I would be taken to my room in a short time. After a few hours, my head had cleared, and I wanted to get up and go for a short walk. I had an IV in my arm. I told the nurse I wanted to get up and walk around. The nurse informed me that I had just had major surgery. I wasn't allowed to get up because the "gash" I had across my stomach had stitches, and it would be a couple of days before I could get up. This was several years before the current new procedures had been developed. Then it was quite common to be in the hospital for one week or more to recover.

I asked the nurse to call the doctor because I wanted to get up and get on with my life. The doctor told the nurse, "If he wants to get up, it's okay with me." So, every hour I got up and walked to the nurses' station down the hall and back to my room. It was quite painful, but having gained hospital experience as an x-ray technician in the Army, I had seen that people who lay around for days would get very stiff. I knew there was a certain amount of pain I would have to endure, but I didn't want the stiffness to set in on me.

When the doctor came in the next morning, he couldn't believe that I had had surgery the day before. He said my complexion looked normal, and he was allowing me to go home that day. It was very unusual to be able to go home the day after gall bladder surgery in those days. When I got home, I was very happy that my surgery had gone well, and I could get on with my life. It almost felt like I had another chance at life. I didn't want to waste one second of it.

After my gall bladder surgery, I realized that I wanted to find the purpose to my life. It was nice that I had the courage to open my own business and make it a success on a small scale. However, I felt there had to be more of a reason for me to exist.

How could I find the very purpose to my life in addition to developing my own soul? What was the real contribution that I could make to mankind during my lifetime?

As I started the journey to find my life's purpose, I realized that it was part of my soul's development to work on developing my very being to a higher state of consciousness.

When I went home and had a chance to reflect on what I had learned from the experience of having the gall bladder surgery, I began to realize that I had always enjoyed helping other people.

How would I know that I was fulfilling the very purpose to my life? At that time I began to take more classes, and I decided to read more books as I began my search for my life's purpose.

I came back from the operation with a completely new outlook on life. I wanted to start on a path to become a kinder person to myself and everyone I came in contact with. Whenever I have a serious decision to make, I put myself back to the vision of the last day of my life and asked myself what would I think about this if it was my last day. It is amazing how my priorities changed. Money and material things didn't mean as much. Did people know how much I loved them? Did I choose to realign my priorities to spend more time with my loved ones and doing the things I really enjoyed? If the answer was yes, then I could die with a smile on my face and a happy heart. From my newly gained perspective, I didn't feel that it was important to gain more money or material possessions. I just no longer worried about it.

As I started to look at myself closer, I realized that God doesn't make any junk! That included me. So I decided to become my best friend instead of my worst enemy. If I made a mistake, I was now able to laugh at myself and not be so serious. I even decided to ask my friends to call me by my nickname instead of my first name. Every time someone called me by my nickname, it reminded me of when I was a young boy and not to be so serious.

There is an old saying, "When the student is ready, the teacher appears." I have found this to be true. The right people called me and gave me guidance to continue to follow my heart. Ever since that day, I began to search for inner peace in my life. My eyes had been opened, and I realized that I had been struggling to find happiness in my life. It wasn't something that someone else could give me. I wasn't going to find it by obtaining material possessions.

Happiness was something I could give to myself in the way that I had decided to live my life. The choice was mine to be happy and enjoy life, or to be unhappy and complain about everything. Don't misunderstand me, I still have problems to deal with every day, but the way I approach them makes me happy. Problems will come up and that is the lesson of life. It's how we deal with them that matters. In life we have spiritual lessons to learn. The path to becoming an enlightened spiritual being is a journey. It's not a race.

If we want to repeat a lesson and not learn from it the first time, it's okay. When you are confronted with a difficult situation, ask yourself what is the spiritual lesson here, and accept the challenge to learn it with love and understanding. That way you can progress and move on to the next lesson to make yourself a kinder and wiser spiritual being.

There is and old saying that a journey of 10,000 miles begins with a single step. Throughout life you can choose to continue to grow spiritually. If you choose not to grow, it's okay because it's up to you. It's something you get to do, not something you have to do.

It is human nature to focus our attention on other people's behavior. However, focusing on others distracts us from our own growth and journey. Everyone has to walk their own spiritual path. When you realize that you are on your own journey, you can learn to focus on your own journey rather than judging other people's path and journey.

Although I had the deathbed vision in 1968, it took me several years to understand the full meaning of the vision. As I went through my daily life, I would get flashbacks to that vision. It helped me deal with the problems that I had.

I started to realize how unimportant most of my problems were. Many problems that I initially thought were important began to seem rather insignificant. I decided that it didn't make sense to waste my time and energy worrying about minor problems.

With my new outlook on life, I had a much easier time deciding what was important to me. Although it took sixteen years from the time of the vision until the time I opened my own store, I credit the vision with giving me the sense of direction and purpose in life to achieve that major dream.

When I have a flashback to that vision of seeing myself on my deathbed thinking back over my life, I am happy that I made the choice to take control of my life.

Chapter 5
FINDING THE PURPOSE
TO MY LIFE

In August 1995, I was at a seminar. During a break, I met a man and woman who had just returned from a trip to Machu Pichu, Peru. They were telling me how much they enjoyed the trip and said I should go because it was part of my life's spiritual journey. The discussion was very interesting, and I entertained the idea of going to Peru. I meditated on it and felt that I was to make this journey. So in October of the same year, I made plans to go with a group. This way we would have a guide and the opportunity to get some inside information about Peru.

I was very excited about the opportunity to visit one of the most spiritual places on Earth. Our group met at the Miami International Airport. There were several people from Central Florida, a large group from Canada and a few people from the East Coast. The group became very friendly in a very short time. It was like we had known each other all of our lives. We were destined to be on this trip together.

Our first stop from Miami was Lima, Peru. We arrived late at night, and by the time we made it through customs, it was on to the hotel because we had to leave early in the morning. The next morning we woke up about 6:00 a.m. because our flight from Lima to Cuzco, Peru was to leave around 9:00 a.m. Upon arriving in Cuzco, Peru we went to our hotel to check in and meet our tour guide. He was from the Amazon jungle and his name was William Huayta. I could tell during our first meeting that he was a very spiritual man. We were long lost brothers in the spiritual sense. That day in Cuzco, he gave a talk that helped me on my spiritual journey.

He told us that we were spiritual eagles from the north and that he was a condor from South America. He said when the eagles from the north meet the condors from the south, a spiritual awakening would begin. It would be a time to go within our beings and develop our souls to become unconditionally loving people. He said one of our greatest purposes in life is to overcome our ego and follow our hearts.

At that very moment, I decided to dedicate the rest of my life to my spiritual journey. I considered my ego to be my mind, and I considered my heart to be my feelings, my gut hunch and/or my intuitive feelings. When I follow my mind I feel tethered to the Earthly plane, but when I follow my feelings, I feel more of a connection to God.

This way of viewing life has simplified my journey for inner peace. It has changed what is important to me. I was glad that I had followed my feelings about the trip to Peru. I was supposed to be there with that group for my soul's development.

The next day we took a train from Cuzco and headed for a town outside Machu Pichu, Peru. The train ride was beautiful as we rode through the valleys and mountains. The people were very humble and spiritual. They made their houses out of mud blocks that they let dry and set up somewhat like we use concrete blocks. The floors in the countryside were dirt. I didn't see any huts with electricity. They had large gardens that they worked every day.

As I looked into their eyes and observed their way of life, I saw nothing except happiness and joy. On one hand they didn't seem like they had much in the way of material possessions. On the other hand, they didn't seem like they needed much to enjoy their lives. When we arrived at our stop, there were a lot of vendors selling their wares. Many were very young, perhaps about ten years old. They were some of the best salespeople I had ever met. To say they were persistent and having fun would be an understatement. They were busy selling jewelry and homemade items such as sweaters, hats and food.

It felt like a very relaxed atmosphere to me. There wasn't a fast pace to life. Everyone seemed to be having fun and enjoying life. We were winding down and adjusting from our travels, trying to adjust to the changes in altitude when we arrived at our hotel. I was pleasantly surprised at how nice the accommodations were.

We were all getting excited about the following day because we would be going up the mountains to Machu Pichu. That evening some people went to the village to enjoy experiencing a dip in the hot springs. I went for a walk in the village and started to adjust to my new surroundings. It took a while to adjust to the high altitude because I needed more oxygen. Since air is thinner in the mountains, I had to breathe more to get the amount of oxygen that I needed. It was wonderful being in a completely different environment. The scenery was beautiful.

After I walked back to the hotel, a group of us sat outside and had a discussion about our spiritual paths. It seemed like we were all supposed to meet there at that time. Though I didn't realize it at the time, the stars, moon and Earth were in an alignment that only happens once every hundred years or so.

That day during my walk, I saw quite a few people from different countries wearing white robes. I was told that they had come from all over the world and were having some kind of spiritual meeting. I don't remember the name of the group, but it was something like "The Chosen 111 People of the Earth." I thought that I was lucky to be at Machu Pichu at this particular time because it was obviously a very special time of year to be there.

When I got up the next morning, I was so excited that I could hardly wait for the bus to take us up the mountain. It was quite a ride up the mountain as there were no guardrails, and it was several thousand feet down to the valley. They didn't have any roads that went straight up or down or around the mountains. They had what they called switch backs. In other words, you would go from side to side and work your way up the mountain. It was a very beautiful ride, but at the same time it was very scary because of the drop off. Sometimes it seemed like we were within a few inches of the very edge of the cliff.

It took quite awhile to get to the entrance to Machu Pichu. Once we were at the entrance, there was a cafeteria, hotel and several ticket booths. There were musicians playing their flutes outside the entrance. As we bought our tickets to enter, we were quite anxious to get to the highest peak inside Machu Pichu, so that we could get an overview of the park. We could take pictures and meditate. Once we arrived inside the park, everyone was making a mad dash to get the best view.

It was quite high and with the change in altitude, it didn't take long for people to begin losing their breath and start feeling the effects of the high altitude. Although I was in fairly good shape, I was feeling some of the effects myself. I was in the front group of people going to the top when I noticed that some of our group had fallen behind. So I decided to go back and make sure that everyone was all right. When I reached the slower group, I noticed that most of them had stopped because of the effects of the altitude. I asked if everyone was okay. A woman who wasn't with our group asked me what my name was because she thought that it was nice that I was more concerned about the stragglers in our group than making it to the top first.

She told me that she would stay with our group of stragglers and make sure they were all right. She said to go ahead and get to the top and take my pictures. I thanked her and continued my climb to the top.

When I reached the top, it was one of the most beautiful sights I had ever seen in my life. The combination of mountains, sky, clouds, and Machu Pichu were a magnificent view. I took some pictures, and then I spent some time to meditate. I asked God to renew my body, mind and spirit. Within a couple of minutes the wind really started to blow, and I stood up and held my hands up to the sky. As I held my hands up to the sky, the winds decreased. All of a sudden, I felt what I would call a tornado like effect go through my being. I knew at that very second that my prayer had been answered. The greatest feeling of love came over my body, and I can't express the appreciation I felt for the gift that I had received. I was glowing from head to toe as the spiritual renewal that I wanted had just happened.

We made our way back down to the park entrance. There I noticed the group of people in white robes entering the park. Someone said they were going to have an all-night ceremony with their leaders. While I observed them, I wondered why they all looked so sad and serious. Why were they here, and why was I here at the same time?

Once we were on the bus and headed back to the hotel, some of our group had become sick from the high altitude. I hoped that once they had some rest that they would recover and be prepared to go back the next day. A group of us met for dinner, and we discussed our day. It was a beautiful evening. There was not a cloud in the sky. It was great to have spent the day in Machu Pichu and have my spiritual renewal happen on the first day. I felt very grateful for the experience.

As I was getting ready to leave the dinner, someone suggested a good night's rest so that we would be prepared for the next day's hike up to the Temple of the Moon. It was quite a hike through some very steep and narrow cliffs. Climbing would be very slow and hard.

I turned in for the night and fell asleep feeling very peaceful and happy. Sometime during the night, I heard a tremendous clap of thunder. It was so loud it woke me up. I went over to the window to see if it was going to rain, but there wasn't a cloud in the sky. It's very unusual to have thunder without any clouds in the sky. Then I remembered the ceremony going on in the park with the people in the white robes. I wondered what they might be doing. Had they been able to manifest the thunder, or was it a freak of nature? I went back to sleep thinking about it.

When I met my group for breakfast, we ran into a doctor that happened to be with our group. She looked worn out as if she hadn't been able to sleep that night. I asked her if she was all right. After she had heard the thunder clap, the park's people sought her assistance because one of the members of "The Chosen 111 People of the Earth" had fallen off a cliff during the middle of the night. She had gone to the village to try to help this man. He was in critical condition. She did what she could, but she didn't think he was going to make it. I asked her if she knew what was going on with the people in the white robes, and why someone would wander around in the dark and fall off a cliff. She had heard of the group and said they were there that week for a special ceremony.

After breakfast, we rode the bus for the uphill trip to Machu Pichu again. When we arrived at the park entrance, the woman I had met the day before said I was supposed to go with her that day. She was the woman who had told me the day before that she would take care of the members of our group that had fallen behind. I had thought that I would be going with our group to the Temple of the Moon, but I left our group and went with the woman.

She was an American who was on a spiritual journey, and she had spent several months in Peru. I asked her what we would be doing that day, and she told me that we were going to the Temple of the Mountains. On the way up to the temple, we went through some holy places such as a cave that she had found and used for meditation. During our hike, she told me about the time she had spent in Peru by herself.

It was quite interesting listening to a woman who had the courage to go to a foreign country by herself with little money and live off the land. She told me how kind the people were and how much she was enjoying her spiritual journey. When we finally got to the Temple of the Mountains, a shaman was waiting for us. It was quite interesting because he spoke Spanish and I didn't. The woman who took me to the temple spoke Spanish, so she became the interpreter for us. The first thing the shaman told me was that we should be grateful for what we have.

Mankind is always asking for more, but never seems to appreciate the things we already have. Such as our health, the water, Mother Earth, food, and the opportunity to develop our souls. The first thing he said we should do is thank the Great God for everything we have. He did this by taking his water and spilling some of it on the ground, back to Mother Earth, to show appreciation before he drank his water.

He pointed to the steps leading up to the Temple of the Mountains. There were three steps. These three steps are a symbol of what we are to accomplish in our lifetime. The first step is to learn to love yourself unconditionally. The second step is to love your fellow man as yourself. The third step is to teach what you have learned by the example that you set. He said it is very important to complete each step before you move on to the next step.

How can you love someone else if you don't love yourself, he asked. How can you teach by example if you don't love your fellow men as yourself? Why does a person need more than his fair share? He said there are many personal challenges to overcome. Gluttony is one of the biggest challenges. Would you share with your neighbor who is less fortunate than you?

We meditated together. He had me sit where kings had sat before. As I meditated, in my mind's eye I became one of the eagles of the north. The spiritual awakening was in progress, and I would do my share to bring the light to mankind. After the prayer, I thanked the shaman for his time and interest in me. As I walked away I thought to myself, what are the chances of my being able to spend a quality afternoon with a shaman and an interpreter all by myself. This wasn't part of the original plan for the day, but it surely was meant to happen. I knew that I was on the right path and felt very good about my decision to visit Peru.

Sometimes different things happen to people. I was definitely on my own journey during this trip. I could have gone with the group on the trip to the Temple of the Moon. Instead, I had a trip that was designed for me. To follow my feelings and leave the group for the day was one of the best decisions I had ever made. I didn't make it happen. I allowed it to happen as it turned out to be for my benefit.

At dinner everyone was talking about their day and wondering what had happened to the man in the white robe who fell off the mountain. I was in such bliss and happiness that I felt that I understood the way to be an enlightened human being. The next few days were wonderful as the group continued to have different experiences during our visit. One thing that we did often was to meditate in different spiritual places. We sang our Oms and definitely raised our vibrations.

The next major event that happened to me during my Peru visit was a seminar presented by Dr. Sharon Forrest. She taught our group how to do a "complete mind and body alignment." This mind and body alignment technique had come to her in a dream. This technique involved two people working as partners, and other people in the room would act as spotters. The purpose of the spotters will be explained later.

The person who wanted to receive a compete mind and body alignment would sit in a chair. They would sit with the back of the chair on either their left or right side rather than covering their back. The other person would volunteer to be the facilitator. The facilitator would place the palms of their hands on the other person's head. One hand would be cupped against the person's forehead and the other hand would be cupped around the lower back part of the person's head covering a part of the back of the head that felt like a "knob." The person receiving the alignment would say a prayer asking for the alignment and giving permission to receive the alignment. The facilitator would say a prayer asking to be a conduit for the complete mind and body alignment. This prayer was the beginning of the alignment.

After the prayer, the facilitator would continue to keep the palms of their hands on the forehead and on the "knob" on the back of the head of the recipient. After a span of time, the recipient would go into a deep meditation or trance. The recipient would eventually relax and "fall" back off the chair as two people acting as spotters would gently ease them to the floor. The recipient would lie on the floor with the facilitator still holding on to the front and back of the recipient's head. The complete mind and body alignment would take about one hour for each person.

Each person had a different experience. No two are alike. Some people would cry and become very emotional, while others would experience nothing. It just depended on what people wanted and what they needed. In my own case, I asked God to give me the complete mind and body alignment with all sincerity and love.

The facilitator put her hands on the front and back of my head. I began to meditate and relax. Before long I was in a state of bliss, and I felt like I was floating on a cloud. I fell back. The spotters caught me and helped me lie flat on the floor. The facilitator kept her hands on my head the whole time.

I was completely relaxed and in a deep meditation, although I knew where I was and what was happening. After a few more minutes, my head started to move from side to side. This was quite interesting because I wasn't moving it. Then after a couple more minutes my head stopped moving, and my left arm started to move. It went up as far as it could stretch, then stretched out and down as far as it could. This continued for a couple of minutes. Then it stopped, and my right arm started to move the same way. This went on for a couple of minutes. When the arm movements stopped, my body without any conscious effort on my part rolled on its side. While I was on my side, my back and chest felt like they were being moved. I could feel each of my vertebrae being adjusted. After my back was done, my left leg moved back and forth for several minutes. Then my left leg stopped, and my right leg went through the same series of movements.

This was a wonderful experience for me. It proved to me the very existence of God because if I wasn't moving my body, who was? There definitely was something moving from one part of my body to another. I wasn't making the movements! I felt so grateful to have had experienced this technique called "The Complete Mind and Body Alignment." It was evident to me that my connection with God was real and manifested itself that day in Peru.

I thanked Dr. Forrest for sharing her dream and technique with us. She told us that when the technique came to her in a dream, she felt it was something that anyone could do, and it was to be shared with everyone.

I was really glad that I had followed my feelings to go on the trip to Peru. The information that I had received has helped me on my life's spiritual journey. It was like the pieces of life's puzzle were starting to come together for me. I no longer wondered if there was life after death. The proof was shown to me in a way that I could understand.

During the Complete Mind and Body Alignment exercise, my body was moving in a very organized fashion. If I wasn't moving my body, who was? It was like being the observer of my own renewal while it was happening.

We had about thirty participants during the Complete Mind and Body technique. It was wonderful to be the one receiving the alignment, but it was also wonderful to be a facilitator and allow the energy from God to flow through me and help someone else. While I was a facilitator, I could see around the room and view the different things happening to the participants.

Some people received the emotional release that they needed, and as a result of this they were crying. Others had no significant experience. During the last part of the workshop, we sat in a circle, and each person was allowed to describe their experience. It was interesting to hear them share their experience. Each person in the room had the opportunity to receive the alignment and to be a facilitator in the alignment of the person who was their facilitator. The overall feeling in the room was a feeling of bliss. How could life get any better? It was such a wonderful feeling to just forget about our problems and start to really feel the true meaning of life.

Everyone in the room was like a family member, and most had received the healing that they had asked for. It may have been an emotional, physical or spiritual healing that was received. I truly believe that I will live a much happier and longer life because of the information that I received on the Peru trip.

The people who went on this trip were great, and our opportunity to share with one another was fantastic. Included in our tour group were several people from Canada that I bonded with. They were friendly and invited me to come to Vancouver, Canada. They even offered me a place to stay. I thought about the invitation and decided to go. I never dreamed that I would be going to Canada two weeks after I returned from Peru.

By having the courage to follow my feelings to go to Peru, I was given the opportunity to continue on my spiritual journey through the connections I made with the Canadians. My comfort zone was expanding as I was able to take advantage of the opportunities life was offering me. I no longer worried about how I was going to pay for another trip. I knew that the resources would be there if I followed my heart.

Chapter 6
THE EMOTIONAL RELEASE

I really felt excited about going to Vancouver, British Columbia to link up with the new friends that I had made on the Machu Pichu trip. Dr. Sharon Forrest had asked me to participate in another seminar she was doing there in November 1995. It would also be a reunion of sorts with the group from Peru. I was able to stay at the home of one of them and really appreciated their efforts to help me during the entire trip.

The first day of the seminar I knew that I was really glad to go with that group. I was excited to see what else I was going to be exposed to for the development of my soul. The first thing we did that had a major impact on me was called "An Emotional Release."

We were assigned a partner to work with. I was assigned to a woman who hadn't been on the Peru trip. It was very interesting because the first thing we did was similar to the Complete Mind and Body workshop. One of us would be the facilitator, and the other would be the recipient. I was the facilitator for the woman I was working with. Then we switched, and I became the recipient. The first thing I did while being the facilitator for her was to put one cupped hand on her forehead and one cupped hand on the back of her head on the area

I call the knob. Then we both said a prayer asking for God's energy to come through the facilitator into the recipient for an emotional release.

The unresolved anger we keep inside creates an unhealthy environment for our body and causes disease. So the idea of the exercise was for the recipient to think about something that really made them mad. It was important to concentrate on one occurrence or one person that made us angry. Then the recipient was asked to state out loud in a strong voice what had made them angry. This was done to get the anger out of their system and to create the emotional release that they were seeking. My partner in this exercise forcibly stated in a loud and angry voice that she hated her mother.

Then the facilitator, which in this case was me, asked her to repeat what she had said. Example: "Who do you hate?" She again stated forcibly, "I hate my mother." Next the facilitator would ask, "Why do you hate your mother?" She said it was because she worked so hard to maintain a straight A average, and her mother never told her how proud she was of her.

From the daughter's perspective, it didn't seem like the mother knew or appreciated how much work and energy she put into her school work. It was difficult for the daughter to understand why her mother didn't acknowledge her achievements in school. During this part of the exercise the recipient, in this case the daughter, would take her anger out on a pillow that was provided. She would pretend that she was talking to her mother as she looked at the pillow. It was very loud. It was very important to get all of that stuffed anger out of her system.

It was exhausting for her, the recipient, to release her anger. She became very emotional and cried. "Mom, why didn't you ever show an interest in what I was doing?" she sobbed. "Why didn't you just love me?" After she had said what she wanted her mother to know and hear her plea for love, it seemed that she had released all her pent-up anger over this issue. This was also a very emotional experience for me as the facilitator. My heart went out to her. The woman pretty much cried herself out, and I gave her a big hug. She smiled because it was good to have the anger out of her system. However, the emotional release wasn't quite over.

During the next step, we pretty much started over as we were told to ask the recipient to become the person that they hated. This was done so that the recipient could see the other side of the picture. The woman I was working with then became her mother. The mother was asked to think about what was bothering her and what she hated. The mother replied in a very loud voice that she hated the fact that her kids didn't appreciate all the work she had to do every day, including the laundry, cooking their meals, keeping the house clean, while working a full-time job. She talked about how exhausted she was when each day was done. No one in the household had appreciated her efforts, and it was very sad from her perspective.

All at once the daughter could understand the mother's viewpoint and see her side of the experience. Her heart went out to the mother, and she understood that the family didn't seem to have the ability to communicate their appreciation to each other. It was no longer that important to the daughter about her school work as she seemed to understand her mother was doing the best that she could. The experience of going through the emotional release had been very good for the daughter. She seemed to understand life and her mother better.

As the facilitator, that experience also helped me as I would be sure to consider both sides of the story in my life's future. I could see by the gleam in the daughter's eye when the emotional release was over how much love she had for her mother. When she became her mother and saw her mother's viewpoint, it changed her whole attitude. Also, she realized she was a participant in her mother's pain. Sometimes, we don't realize that the problems we are experiencing are built up in our mind's eye like making a mountain out of a mole hill. We could stop and ask ourselves is this a major problem, or am I making a big deal out of something small?

Another recipient in the group was a man on the other side of the room. He was so far away, so I only caught a little of one experience that he had. I didn't have the opportunity to work with or talk to this man, but I did overhear a small part of what happened to him. He was a small child, and he was telling a man to get off him. Evidently, when he was a child he had been molested by a man. My heart went out to him, and I realized that some people really do have major issues to work out in their life.

The problems that I felt that I had with my parents were just a part of my life's experience. I now know that both of my parents did the best they could, and I love them both very much. They both have passed on, and I really appreciate their participation in my life's journey. I wouldn't have anyone else for parents because the experiences that I have gone through with them have developed me to the point that I am today.

I still have plenty to experience and learn. I am just more open to my spiritual growth and the lessons that it will bring me. After the seminar was over, most of the group from the Peru trip had dinner together. It was nice to be in their company for these few days. The next day I was taken to the airport to return home. The lady who took me to the airport said she was supposed to give me a book. It was *The Greatest Miracle in the World* by Og Mandino. By following her feeling to give me the book, she has helped me put another piece of my life's puzzle in place.

I found the *The Greatest Miracle in the World* to be very significant in my personal development. "The God Memorandum" in this book is a message from God to us. It helped me appreciate my very being. I couldn't put the book down. It was so simple, but so true. Sometimes we forget to count our blessings. We forget that we have the power to choose. We can choose to love, or we can choose to hate. When we choose to love, it completes the circle of life. For only by giving can we truly receive.

By following my feeling and going on the trip to Canada, I was starting to realize that most of the experiences that I have gone through were for my own personal development. I realized that each person has their own issues to deal with. It doesn't matter if you are rich or poor, life will offer you lessons to learn. It's our attitude, and how we look at these opportunities that shape our development.

I decided to enjoy each day and meet the daily challenges with a smile and open heart. I began to see others in a completely different light. I realized that everyone is dealing with their own particular life experiences in the best way they know how. I would try to see their side of our joint lessons in life as I tried to improve the way I looked at each of the experiences I had with them. It made each lesson a lot easier to tolerate knowing that the ball was in my court for half of the experience.

How could someone fight with me if I didn't want to fight with them? It was no longer important who was right or wrong as I looked at it as a lesson for both of us.

Most of the time we were both right as we looked at it from our own perspective. It was a good feeling to be able to develop the ability to confront without conflict. In other words, I could become the observer in the particular lesson and state my side as I saw it while considering the other person's viewpoint. I didn't have to win the discussion or particular lesson. Being able to overcome the urge to take the experience personally was a great step toward becoming an enlightened human being. Instead of having a knot in my stomach, I felt at peace with each occurrence. I would no longer become upset inside of me because I didn't like the way that would make me feel, and I knew that the stress would be bad for my health.

Now that I have changed my outlook on life, as I look back over my life I see how many people have influenced my development. When I was about twelve years old, I was at a diner with a friend who was thirteen. My friend got into an argument with the man who was sitting at the counter in the diner. As I tried to smooth things over between the two of them, my friend left without me. I stayed and got into a discussion with the man sitting beside me at the counter. He was a complete stranger to me. I told him my life's story up to that point in time. Perhaps it reminded him of his own childhood, because he developed tears in his eyes, and he gave me encouragement. I was a complete stranger to him, but I could feel his love and compassion for me as a fellow human being.

As he left the diner, he gave me a twenty-dollar bill and wished me luck. I never saw him again, but he played a part in my spiritual development. This happened in the winter of 1954 in Greenville, Pennsylvania. Twenty dollars was a lot of money back then. At that time, I could go to a movie for twenty-five cents.

I was very appreciative of the gift and have never forgotten his generosity. This is an example of how we can help each other in life. I have tried to pass on his kindness and generosity in my life.

The argument between my friend and this complete stranger is an example of how life's lessons are brought to us. How could the same guy who was so kind to me be so argumentative with my friend? My buddy took their discussion personally, and as a result they raised their voices and became involved in an unpleasant confrontation. When my friend found out that the complete stranger had given me twenty dollars, he couldn't believe it. This was an example to me of how the same situation can have a completely different outcome. People are basically good and want to do the right thing.

Chapter 7
SPIRITUAL LESSONS

I have written about some of the spiritual lessons that I have experienced in my life. It is my hope that we can learn from each other's personal experiences. Sometimes we may not understand the spiritual lesson at the time we are going through it. These lessons are for the overall development of our soul.

The opportunity to forgive one another with unconditional love is part of our life's journey. I have written examples of some of my experiences to demonstrate how things don't always go as planned. In no way am I trying to say how to handle each example shown. There are many ways to handle each of life's lessons.

SPIRITUAL LESSON #1: CAREER CHOICES
When I was a teenager in high school in Greenville, Pennsylvania, we used to sit around and gripe about the fact that we were tired of the little town we grew up in. Around 1960, the town had been written up as being one of the best towns to grow up in Pennsylvania. There was a park with ball fields, a swimming pool, an artificial ice skating rink, and a recreation center. All of these facilities were within a block of my house. My buddies and I wanted to see the outside world. We were bored with liv-

ing in a small town. We didn't know how good we had it.

I was a poor kid as far as money and material possessions go. However, I was supported by a wonderful community with plenty to do if I had chosen to do it. I had several opportunities during my senior year in high school to go to college. I even had a doctor who offered to pay my way through college if I would buckle down and study.

One day a couple of my buddies were going to talk to the Air Force recruiter, and they asked me if I wanted to go with them. I said sure and went along for the ride. By the time we arrived, the Air Force recruiter had gone to lunch. So we went over and talked to the Army recruiter. The next thing I knew, we planned to go into the Army on the buddy plan. One of my friend's mother was a nurse, and she thought we should be x-ray technicians because it was a nice clean job. It sounded good, and we could use what we learned in the Army in civilian life. Also, we liked the idea that the three of us would be going through Army training and x-ray school together.

The school would last about one year with basic training. Becoming a medic was a requirement before x-ray school. We never considered the fact that we might not all have the same aptitude and abilities. So we took our aptitude tests, and I was the only one to qualify for x-ray school. Our plan to be together was shattered, but we still had to go into the Army.

I was on my own because our schools started at different times. I didn't think much about what a big change I was in for. I remember the day I went to be sworn into the Army. They were very nice to us before we were sworn in. As we were getting ready to be sworn in the sergeant asked, "Is there anyone here that wants to chicken out?" I wondered to myself who is going to chicken out? I knew it wouldn't be me. Then we were sworn in, and the going got a lot rougher.

The first thing he said after we were sworn in was that we were a bunch of filthy pigs. The place was a mess, and he started our training by screaming at the top of his lungs at us. In less than one minute, I knew that I had made a terrible mistake. I went from wanting to leave my home to being homesick in the span of about one minute. I had signed up for three years in the regular Army, which meant that I wanted to be there. There was no way that I could get of it with honor. I hadn't done my homework to find out what I was getting myself into.

The point of this example is the importance of getting as much information about your life choices as you can. For example, I could have joined the Army Reserves for six-month active duty to see if I liked it or not. That way after six months I could go on with my civilian life if I didn't like it, or I could sign up after the six months to stay in longer if I did like it.

How many young men realize what they are getting themselves into when they make that type of decision. How many seventeen-year-old boys went to war after three to six months of training? Some of them never made it back. They went from one extreme to the other.

If this was what they wanted, it's fine. But how much thought did they put into it? What decision would they make while being in a foxhole with someone shooting at them trying to kill them? Who really wants to be put into the position to kill or be killed? The military is just one example of extremes. If you try it and you like it, great!

This example is presented to help you make certain that you don't put yourself into a situation that you want to get out of but can't. If a decision you are making will involve several years of your life, make sure that you do a lot of careful investigating and planning. It is very important to make informed decisions because your very life may depend on it.

SPIRITUAL LESSON #2: THE TRUCK

I hired a mechanic at my business. He was from Baltimore, Maryland and had moved to Florida with his girlfriend. He seemed to be a good mechanic and worked hard at the store. I really appreciated his good work ethic. One day he told me that he was having trouble getting to work because he didn't have adequate transportation. I offered to sell him a truck that I owned for $1,000. He told me that he didn't have any money, but asked me if I could take fifty dollars a week out of his paycheck. I agreed to do so and signed over the title to him. I didn't put a lien on the title for the amount he still owed me.

The fifty dollars a week was taken out of his check the first week, and then I never saw him again. I became angry for a moment and thought I would take some action against him. It didn't seem right that he would do this to me. As I thought about it, I started to realize that it was one of my life lessons. He needed the truck more than I did. Evidently, he was homesick or had some type of problem that he had to go back up north.

In my mind's eye, I decided to give him the truck and not let it bother me anymore. I felt bad because he had never said good-bye or explained the reason why he left. He never made another payment on the truck or any effort to contact me.

I decided in my heart to wish him well and forgive him. I understood that sometimes in life you do things you aren't proud of, but this is how we learn. I know that someday when he can that he will help someone else in need, and I can live with that.

SPIRITUAL LESSON #3: THE PRODUCE BUSINESS

Another experience occurred when I decided to help someone in need. This person required assistance because he needed a place to live and some type of work. I loaned him $750 to get an apartment. He said that he knew the produce business and had connections with several produce departments at grocery store chains.

I knew that he had worked in the produce business because he used to come to my store selling strawberries. So we rented a truck, and I went with him to South Florida to buy produce. The idea was that I would provide the cash, and he would provide the knowledge and connections for the produce business. We bought a truckload of produce and headed back to Central Florida.

The next day, he took the truckload of produce around to his connections. I didn't know it at the time, but he had never informed his connections that he was coming by that day with produce to sell. Most of the businesses had already made commitments to someone else for their produce needs. He was able to sell some of the produce, but not all of it.

He didn't show up to see me for several days. I had thought he had become discouraged and was out spending some of my seed money with his girlfriend, having a good time. After several days, he returned the truck to me with the balance of the produce still in the truck. Most of it was spoiled and had to be thrown away. When he gave me some money from the proceeds that he had collected, he apologized for wasting some of the money with his girlfriend.

I was then stuck with the task of disposing of the spoiled produce and paying for the rental of the truck. He then told me he would repay the money that I had loaned him for the apartment and the remaining money that he had spent on his girlfriend. The total came to about $1,500. I felt his word was good.

People who knew him said I was stupid for helping him because he would never repay me. Something inside of me wanted to help him, and I followed my feelings instead of following my brain or ego. There was a big possibility that I might never see my money, but I couldn't live with myself if I didn't try to help him.

When it came time to repay me from his disability check, he disappeared and I never saw him. He had been avoiding me and finally he moved out of town. Many people who knew him and had warned me about him gave me the "I told you so." However, in my heart I knew that I had to help him because it was more about my feelings to do the right thing than to follow my brain and deny him assistance. You see there were two parts to this story.

If I gave him the money with unconditional love out

of wanting to help him, how could I turn my back on him? I had to be true to myself and give up the attachment to the unconditional love. Then what he did with the money was part of his soul's development. It wasn't up to me to judge him. I am sure that he would have paid me back if he could have. I never received the money back from him, but I did have an audit on my business insurance policy during that time. As a result of the audit, I received a check from the insurance company for about $3,000. This $3,000 was double the amount that the man owed me. I knew in my heart that it was God's way of thanking me for helping someone in need. I felt good about what I had done, and how I had the strength to follow my heart.

SPIRITUAL LESSON #4: COSTA RICA TRIP

One day I received a phone call from my store in DeLand, Florida. I was informed that a customer wanted me to call her. She wanted to know if I would be interested in going to Costa Rica to help her determine if she and her husband should open a rental store in San Jose, Costa Rica.

She said they would put my wife and me up at their home in San Jose and provide our meals. All we would have to pay was our round trip airfare.

I had always wanted to visit Costa Rica. I discussed the woman's offer with my wife, and we decided to go. I figured it would be an interesting trip, and I was excited about visiting a new country.

When we arrived in San Jose, it was quite different from what I had expected. I had envisioned a tropical paradise with people relaxing in the sun and enjoying life. Instead, what I found was a very large city with tremendous traffic jams. There was barbwire and fencing around most of the homes. Guards with rifles were in front of most of the businesses. These aspects of the country were rather frightening to me.

When we arrived at the woman's neighborhood, it was surrounded by a brick wall with razor wire around the top. Also, there were armed guards at the gated entrance to the neighborhood. There were only about seven or eight houses in her development, which was built into the side of a large hill.

The woman we were staying with had raved about how inexpensive it was to live in Costa Rica. She stated that the wages there very low, around one to two dollars per hour. Her home was quite pretty, but it did not have air conditioning. She had a housekeeper and a driver. Her housekeeper spoke virtually no English, and her driver spoke some English.

The woman we were staying with had said she hadn't seen any rental stores in her area. She asked her driver if he knew of any equipment rental stores, and he said he did not. She felt that a rental store in her area would be very successful because there was a need for that type of service. As far as she could see no one was filling this need. She had looked in the Yellow Pages under rental and had not found any listings.

The Yellow Pages were in Spanish, which is the official language of Costa Rica. My wife looked up the word rent in an English-Spanish dictionary. Then she looked that word up in the Yellow Pages and found several listings for rental stores. The next couple of days, the woman's driver took us to several of the rental stores in her area, and we discovered plenty of excellent rental stores. At that point, the woman realized that opening a rental store there was not the opportunity that she had thought it would be.

That evening we had a long discussion with this woman about rental stores and difficulties she had faced in her life. Her husband was working in Saudi Arabia and had been there for several years. He was making excellent money and was planning on retiring to Costa Rica. He had wanted to operate his own business, and that is why they had come up with the idea for a rental store.

The woman started to tell me about some of the difficult things she had been through in the past few years. A few years prior to this her husband had developed a serious heart condition and was told that he might not have long to live. At this time, their son had just turned sixteen. Facing the possibility of dying, the man felt that it was important to him to see his son get his driver's license as soon as possible and have a really nice car. To him a nice car would be a brand new sports car. Shortly after that the son completed his driver's training and received his driver's license. While the man was still in the hospital recuperating, his wife went out and bought the son an expensive sports car.

Shortly after buying the car, the son complained that he had a problem steering it. They took the car back to the dealership for repairs. A few days later, the son and a female friend were out driving, and he crashed the car into a tree. Both the son and his friend died as a result of the crash.

His parents were filled with grief and guilt over the death of their son and his friend. They blamed themselves for the deaths because they were the ones that bought the son the car.

When the woman told me about her son's death, I realized the purpose of my trip to Costa Rica. I felt I was there to try and help her with her grief and guilt over the loss of her son. The trip didn't have anything to do with the opening of a rental store after all.

What can you tell someone who has been through such a difficult experience? Sometimes terrible things happen that are beyond our control. There really isn't much we can do to prevent them. Life is to be lived in the moment we are in because we never know what tomorrow will bring.

I don't know if I helped ease the woman's pain during my stay in Costa Rica. However, the events in her life were a real eye opener for me. I decided I would no longer let minor problems upset me.

Sometimes we have to develop our soul under very difficult circumstances. Can we learn to forgive ourselves when something bad happens even though we had only the best intentions?

The point is that the lessons never stop. Why would we let little problems upset us? Sometimes the lessons are major, and it takes all of our will power and heroic persistence to get through them.

I think that we should learn to appreciate each day and not take it for granted. Sometimes life doesn't go as you have planned. As difficult as it can be, life is a school, and we are the students.

The ability to appreciate each experience helps the development of our soul. To know the real feeling of love is a blessing in itself. When you have the feeling of the love of yourself for no reason, you have raised your vibration to a higher level.

SPIRITUAL LESSON #5: THE FATHER'S WILL

I am an auctioneer and do estate sales occasionally. During 2003, I received a call from a woman who asked me to do an appraisal on her dad's furniture and household items located in Sanford, Florida. Her father had passed away, and her family couldn't agree on the value of his belongings.

I asked her on the phone to tell me what she had and how old it was. After she described the items to me, I said the appraisal would cost around $300, and I didn't think that the items she described to me would be worth much more than the $300 appraisal fee. She told me to come over and do the written appraisal because she and her two brothers couldn't agree on the value of her father's items.

I went to her father's house and examined his household furnishings. I again told her that the houseful of items would have an auction value of a little more than $300.

I suggested rather than pay for a written appraisal which would cost $300, she and her brothers should get together and agree on a price for each individual item. They would write their names on a slip of paper, and put the names in a hat. Then they would draw the slips of paper out of the hat to determine the order of which one of them would get to pick the first $100 worth of items. The next person would pick $100 worth of items and so on with the third person. They would take turns picking items until all of the items were gone. She would save the $300 appraisal fee.

After I suggested this to her, we became involved in a spiritual discussion and talked about some of the principles discussed in this book. Later, she said the real reason she called me was that her dad had left over $700,000 in cash to her and one of her brothers.

Her dad had left nothing in his will to the other brother because the two of them did not get along. This brother had in the past borrowed $100,000 from his mother, who had been divorced from the father for several years. This son had never made any attempt to repay his mother the $100,000 loan. He had a large, fancy, expensive house, new expensive vehicles and lived beyond his financial means.

The father's will clearly stated that this brother was excluded from receiving any of the father's money. The sister wanted to do the right thing, and she asked me if they should split the money three ways, or follow the father's wishes and exclude the brother from any of the money. I told her that it was her choice to decide what to do with the money. She was within her rights to exclude him per the will.

However, she was afraid that if she did exclude her brother, he would never forgive her, and it would divide the family even more. She just couldn't figure out what was the right thing to do and sought my advice. I said that I couldn't tell her what to do, but if this day was the last day of her life, what would she have wished she had done? I told her to think about it from that perspective, and whatever she decided would be fine.

A few days later, I received a phone call from her. She told me that she had talked to the brother who was listed in her father's will to receive half of his estate. They had decided that family was more important than money, so they agreed to split the money three ways and include the other brother. They were happy because this experience had brought their family closer together.

The brother who had originally been excluded from the estate later repaid their mother the $100,000 that he owed her. The sister said when she and her brother had looked at the problem from the perspective of the last day of their lives, they wanted to have a smile on their face knowing that they had done the right thing. She also said they felt that their father had used me to get them to open their hearts and include the brother in his will. Even though the brother and the father didn't get along during the last part of the father's life, he loved all of his children.

This is an example of how wonderful people can be once we put ego aside and follow our heart. We can make a difference in this world when we follow our heart.

SPIRITUAL LESSON #6: LET GO AND LET GOD

The past few years business had really become tough. Previously I had expanded my business to a total of three stores. As we got more competition, I decided to sell one of the stores. It was just a thought that I had in my mind's eye. I hadn't listed it with any real estate companies or business brokers. One day I got a call from a man who was interested in buying the property, but he wasn't interested in buying the business or the equipment.

My original thought was to keep the property, but sell the rental business and lease the property to the purchaser of the business. I told him that I would lease him the property. But he really wasn't interested in leasing. So the deal seemed to fall through.

I thought about it for a couple of months. I tried to figure out how I would come out with the sale of the equipment if I liquidated the business and sold the property. After doing that, I changed my mind, and I called the man back. I told him that I would sell him the property if I could get my asking price. He said that he would think about it and get back to me.

After doing some checking into the prices of property in the area, he made such a low offer that I wasn't interested in taking it. I told him I couldn't sell it to him for that price. The deal seemed dead in the water again.

After a couple more months, he made me an offer that was several thousand dollars below my asking price. I refused to accept his offer. So once again the deal seemed doomed because I wanted to get a price that I thought was fair, taking into consideration that I would have to liquidate the business and equipment. I felt the business had more value than its liquidation value because the store had been in business about twenty-five years.

As I continued to try and figure out a way to make the deal work, I got the message in a meditation to go ahead and sell the property for the price he had offered even though it was considerably less than the amount I wanted for the property.

I decided to follow my feelings to let go, and let God handle the situation. Therefore, I made the decision to go ahead and sell the property. I hated to sell the property for several thousand dollars below my asking price, but I called him. I said that I had decided to take his offer for the property. He agreed, and we signed a contract. I was glad to be getting this deal done because I had some bills I wanted to pay off and improve my cash flow. I had a dollar figure in mind as to how much money I would raise by liquidating the equipment. To my pleasant surprise, I received more from the liquidation of the equipment than I anticipated. The increased amount that I received from the equipment sale was twice the amount that I thought I had lost by taking a lower price for the property.

This showed me that God had a plan that would benefit me, but I just didn't understand it at the time. When I decided to let go and let God, it was a wise decision. I followed my heart (my feelings) instead of being stuck with my ego (my mind). By doing so, I received more money than I had originally anticipated.

This was another example of how when I follow my feelings, things seem to work out for the best, even though I might not understand it at the time. The key is that I don't have to understand it. I just have to have the courage to follow my heart.

SPIRITUAL LESSON #7: THE DOME EXPERIENCE

One day I went to "The Dome" in Beverly Beach, Florida to look around and see what was going on there. I had been there before and had taught some seminars there. The Dome had been founded by Frank Shore. He had developed it from the ground up to be an alternative healing center. His first two wives had both died of cancer, and he was looking for a cure.

One of the rooms in the dome was called the crystal room. The room was filled with crystals, and people would meditate in it. Usually they would have at least seven people to do a group meditation. That afternoon ten of us participated in a group meditation.

Most of the people in the group were strangers to me. After about ten minutes of meditation, I had the urge to allow the message that was coming through me to speak. So I started to talk while I was in a light trance. I didn't think about what I was saying. I just allowed whatever feelings I had to be expressed to the group. The message that was given through me lasted for about fifteen minutes.

I felt like my higher self or my connection to God was coming through me to the group. It was a good feeling to have the confidence to just allow the message to flow through me while being with a group of strangers. After the group meditation was over, I was wondering why this had happened, since I wasn't judging it or anything. I guess it was just a message for the group.

It didn't take long to find out. A lady asked me if I would take a moment to talk with her. She had tears in her eyes as she told me that before she went into the group meditation, she had said a prayer asking for help in her life's situation. The words I had spoken during the meditation had given her the answers that she had asked for in her prayer.

This really had an impact on me because I realized that I was being used to help other people. It was a very humbling experience for me. At the same time it was reassuring to know that I was on the right track, allowing the message to flow through me. My message had

had some real meaning, and it was nice to have it confirmed. I was glad that I had followed my feelings to go to the dome that day. It helped me realize my purpose in life was to develop my own soul to the extent that other people would also be helped even if I didn't realize it while it was happening. Doing what I call my spiritual work is my first priority and the purpose to my life.

SPIRITUAL LESSON #8:
THE CIRCLE OF LIFE HEALING SESSION

I had been asked by a personal friend to participate in a hands-on healing session for a man who had terminal cancer. The man had lost a tremendous amount of weight and was at the end of his life. When we arrived, it was obvious that he had only a few more days to live. As I began to talk with his family, I could see the love that they had for him. My heart went out to them. Little did I realize that this was another opportunity for me to expand my wisdom of life.

As I began the hands-on healing for him, I prayed for God's love to flow through me and into him to help him in his passing over to the other side. I could feel the healing energy flowing through me and into him. He was either in a coma or resting when I started working on him.

My part of the healing session continued for about thirty minutes. All of a sudden, the man reached up with his hand and grabbed a hold of my arm. His eyes opened up, and as he looked into my eyes he said, "I love you." This had a huge impact on me and startled me because I was in a meditative state during the healing.

Somehow I felt that God was using him to heal me at the same time that I was working on healing this man. This experience helped me understand the circle of life as it relates to love.

When we are born, we love everyone unconditionally without judgment. Then we go through the trials and tribulations of life's lessons in order to develop our soul. When we are completing our journey in this life, we are to develop our souls to the point of being an unconditionally loving person. When we leave this life, we are back to the point where we came into this life. Thus we complete the circle of life. The experience I had that day really helped me understand the circle of life.

Chapter 8
THE JUDGMENT DAY VISION

I went to a seminar a few years ago in Oviedo, Florida that opened my mind's eye to another vision that had a huge impact on my life. The facilitator started off the seminar by telling us to approach the exercises and meditations without any fears.

The example she gave was that if during the meditation we were standing at the edge of a cliff like the Grand Canyon, we should not be afraid to stretch ourselves out and jump off the cliff. She said the courage to jump off the cliff would take us deeper into our meditation and help us release our fears. I had never tried to stretch myself out like this before. She led us in a group meditation about releasing our fears.

As I started my meditation, I started to relax and connect with the wonderful bliss that meditation brings to me. I felt like I was floating on a cloud just feeling the love of the universe and soaking in the warmth and tenderness. After a few minutes, I jumped off the cloud into the depths below. I was soaring like an eagle and enjoyed it very much. This was a different experience than in other meditation in which I was trying to find peace and happiness by using every ounce of my strength to climb the ladder of life and seek wisdom. In those meditations and in life, I had held onto the ladder of wisdom so tightly that it was difficult to move because each step up was quite hard and a struggle.

When I had the courage to jump off the cloud, it was like letting go of my grip on the ladder. I had made the decision to go for it. To my pleasant surprise, instead of falling down from the ladder, I went up the ladder without realizing I had been holding myself back from the progress that I was seeking.

By holding on to the ladder of wisdom so tightly, I was restricting my spiritual growth without realizing it. When I had the courage to follow my feelings and jump off the cloud, I finally released the chains that bound me. I was free to soar with the eagles of the north. It was a wonderful feeling, and I didn't have a care in the world. I felt wonderful and connected to God's love more fully than I had ever felt before in my life.

After enjoying this newly found freedom and the loss of all fear, I found myself in a big city in my meditation. I was walking down a street, and everyone was running away from something. Cars were speeding through red lights. Everyone was scattering as quickly as they could. I wondered to myself what was going on. Everyone was in such a state of fear. What was happening that had everyone so shook up? The whole city was in a state of turmoil. I was concerned for the people's state of mind and safety

Cars continued to pass me on the street at a high rate of speed as I walked down the street. I tried to ask people what was happening. After doing this for several minutes, a young man yelled from the back of a car, "Run, today is judgment day!" I heard what he said, but I was somewhat confused.

If it really was judgment day, where did he think that he was going to be able to run? Didn't the people realize that there was nowhere they could hide to get away from their fears? I continued to walk down the street, feeling sad for my fellow man. After a while, I felt someone put their arm around me. It was a warm, nurturing presence that I felt. This presence asked me,

"Why is everyone running? What are they afraid of?"

I explained that one of them told me that today was judgment day and they were scared.

After listening to this He said, "What are they afraid of and why are they scared?"

I said they weren't able to live the perfect life that was required of them by some of our teachings. They had all made mistakes in their lives. They're afraid of the punishment and banishment that they thought they would receive.

He asked me why I wasn't running away, and why wasn't I scared?

I replied, "My God is a God of love, and I know how much He loves me. Therefore, I am not afraid of Him."

"Why don't they know how much I love them?" He asked. Then He asked me if I would go with him to do the so-called Judgment Day.

I said that I would go and appreciate the opportunity to learn more about God's judgment. The first place we went to was the worst prison a person could imagine. People had been locked away like animals, and conditions were terrible. It was very dark and gloomy to me.

The first person we saw was in solitary confinement because he had committed murder. He was on death row for his crime against man. The prison door swung open, and we walked into the man's cell. The man had tears in his eyes because he was afraid to meet his Maker.

Suddenly, I could feel God's love fill the room. It was like the love of a mother who has just been reunited with her long lost son. As a mother loves her son unconditionally, God loves every one of us unconditionally.

As God spoke to the man in prison, it was very clear to me that God's love is truly unconditional. God said the prisoner had made a split second decision that had changed his life. In a moment of anger, the man had lost his temper and killed someone. According to man's law, he would have to be held responsible for the act that he had committed. He had affected the lives of many people by his loss of control.

God said, "I can only watch as I gave you free will to

use your power of choice. Use your power of choice wisely. Choose to love, not to hate. Choose to build, not to destroy. Never demean yourself again as you are my greatest joy. I watch your spirit grow with the circumstances of your life. Choose to forgive one another as I will forgive you because of my unconditional love for each one of you."

The next place we went to was a cave where people with terrible diseases lived. We observed how well they were working together and taking care of each other. You could see the unconditional love that they had for each other. Although they had few worldly possessions, each one of them seemed to have a glow around them.

As we watched them, I would feel the Father's pride and unconditional love for His children. I never saw Him, but it was like I could feel Him with every fiber of my being. He said His love never ends under any circumstances. He asked me if I would go and tell people how much He loves each and every one of us.

"Tell them I will never turn my back on them under any circumstance. I created you, so why would I not be there when your life is over? I will be there for you when you have learned the lessons of life. It's your choice to ascend during your life and become one of my angels on Earth. Choose to become an extension of my unconditional love for each one of you. When you love your fellow man as yourself, there is no greater way to show your love for me. When you help your fellow man, you are helping me. How could I do any less for each and every one of you?"

I told Him that I would carry the message as He asked me to do.

YOUR PERSONAL RELATIONSHIP WITH GOD

How is your personal relationship with God? Do you pray and meditate every day? Does God answer your prayers in a way that you understand? Do you think that God is still active and helping us when we ask for help? Did He stop giving us messages over two thousand years ago? Do miracles still occur?

I think our answer would vary based on our personal relationship with Him.

If you don't pray and meditate, how do you communicate with God? If you do pray and don't meditate, how do you expect God to answer you? Do you think God works for you when you ask to receive something, or do you think God would prefer to work with you? Is it true that you can only see God in another individual to the extent that you know God in your own life?

Do we have our priorities in order? Are we here to develop our own soul, or should we be pointing out the flaws in other people? If my attention isn't on my own personal development, how can I improve my own relationship with God? Are you always looking for what is wrong with everything, or can you see the beauty that is all around us?

Is you personal relationship with God something you experience every Sunday or whenever you can get around to it? Do you walk your talk, living it every day? Are you a reflection of God's love and understanding every day in everything that you do?

If your personal relationship with God isn't quite what you want it to be, how would you begin to put your priorities in order to correct it? Would we begin to make the choice to get our priorities in order? Whose soul are you responsible for anyway?

SELF-ASSESSMENT QUESTIONNAIRE

Have you awakened and taken control of your life?

Did you decide what is important to you?

Did you make a life plan?

What message are you sending to your body, your very being?

Can you see the purpose to some of the events that have happened to you in your life?

Have you started the journey to overcome your ego and follow your heart?

Can you see the other person's viewpoint?

Can you confront without conflict? Do you have to be right?

Are you holding yourself back in the personal development of your soul by being afraid to let go of your ego and follow your heart and feelings?

Can you see the good in everyone?

Have you fallen in love with your own life?

Will you be happy today and enjoy every moment of your life?

Chapter 9
THE AWAKENING EXERCISE

Our purpose in life is to develop our soul and to find our unique talent to help mankind. We go through many lessons in life to bring our awareness in line with our life's purpose. Each person is special and on their own path.

The question is while we are on our spiritual path, how do we know what our unique talent is? What would you do today if you could do anything that you wanted? The answer would be to do the thing you love to do and not to be concerned about material possessions. Here is an exercise to help clear your mind.

THE "LAST DAY OF YOUR LIFE" EXERCISE

Write down your thoughts for each of the following questions below. Use a separate piece of paper if necessary. *Imagine that today is the last day of your life.*

Relax and think back over your life. There is no need to rush through this exercise. Analyze your life and how you feel about the things that have happened in your life as you answer the following questions:

Did you enjoy your life?

Were you able to love yourself unconditionally?

Did you become your best friend?

What do you think about the way you lived your life?

Did you find inner peace in your life?

Were you kind?

Did you hold a grudge against anyone?

If so, what was the reason for the grudge?

Was it that important?

Were you able to forgive them?

Were you able to forgive yourself?

Did you spend enough time with your family?

Does your mother know how much you love her?

Does your father know how much you love him?

Does the rest of your family know how much you love them?

Do you wish you had more material possessions?

Do you wish you had more time?

Did you find the purpose to your life?

What would you change?

There may be some other questions that you would like to ask yourself. If so, relax and ask what else is important to you. After you have read each question and had time to think about it, sit down and write down what was really important to you.

Up to this point in your life, do you think that your priorities are in the correct order or are there things that you would do differently? How would you do it?

Write it down because this is what is important to you. This can help you develop your own road map to inner peace.

Chapter 10
TAKE INVENTORY
OF YOURSELF

The purpose of the awakening exercise is to create a wake up call to the purpose of our lives. Are we drifting in the river of life or have we become the wise master of our soul's development?

For some people, this awakening to life comes after someone close to them dies or when they are confronted with a serious illness.

The purpose of this book is to help you determine what is important in your life. No one can make that decision for you.

TAKING INVENTORY EXERCISE QUESTIONS

What would you do if you had only 30 days to live?

What would you do if you had one year to live?

What will you think of your life when you are lying on your deathbed?

Will you wish you had another chance at life?

What changes would you make?

Are you doing what you love to do?

Is life a pleasure? Are you enjoying every experience?

Are you putting off being happy until tomorrow or have you learned life's lesson to be happy today because today is all we have?

Do you have your priorities in order? Are you working to live or are you living to work?

Do you understand the lessons brought to you by the different people in your life?

Have you developed the ability to forgive people and not judge them?

Can you see that there are two sides to every story?

Are you following your feelings or are you stuck in your ego?

Are you able to live life without fear?

Do you work on your thoughts and look at things in a positive manner?

Can you see the good people all around you?

Do you "Do unto others as you would have them do unto you?"

Can you become the light and be a mentor for others to follow you by the example that you set by your actions?

Have you developed the ability to use your power of choice wisely?

Did you make a life plan?

Have you decided to go for your dreams?

Is life's journey inside of you or is it controlled by events and people in the outside world?

Are you working on your personal relationship with the god force that lives inside of you?

Have you developed the ability to become the observer in your own life?

Do you participate with life? Ships are safer in the harbor, but is that what ships are for?

Do you meditate every morning to put your day in order?

Can you laugh at yourself and not take things too seriously?

Have you found your smile and zest for life?

Can you see the connection between your thoughts and your health?

Are you able to leave each situation feeling good inside instead of being stressed?

Do you appreciate your body in a way it can understand?

Do the people around you know how much you love them?

What do you think is the purpose of your life?

Are you focusing on the things that are really important to you?

Do you know what is important to you?

Have you ever thought about it?

Do you want to take control of your personal development?

If you don't do it now, do you think that you ever will?

Does it matter either way?

Are you happy with your life?

What would make you happy?

Do you believe there is more to life than what you are doing currently?

Do you worry a lot about things beyond your control?

Do you want to become the wise master of your soul's development?

Our time on Earth is one of the most valuable things that we have. Shouldn't we enjoy every moment of our life? Who knows how long our life will be? Isn't it important to do what we love to do every day?

DEVELOPMENT OF THE SOUL

We are here because we chose to come to the Earth plane to continue the development of our soul. Each soul picks their particular situation in this lifetime. As a result of this we can work on the particular traits that we want to improve. Each life is designed to allow the soul a myriad of choices for development. Realizing that we are responsible for our own soul's development, we can put more thought into the choices that we make.

Before we can heal the whole world, we are told to heal ourselves first. We have the choice to ascend and become angels on Earth through our power of choice, or we can create hell in our own mind's eye. It is up to each person to decide their own path.

When we realize that our very thoughts create our own reality, we can become wiser human beings. The journey to find ourself is within our hearts and not in the exterior world. The old saying, "No matter where you go, you have to take yourself with you" applies. The secrets of developing your soul and finding happiness lie within you rather than in the outside world. Once we know where to start looking, we can begin to find the peace and happiness that we are seeking.

True happiness isn't something that someone else can give to you. It is something that you give yourself. It's the way that you decide to live your life. We must learn to look at each situation as an experience to learn and develop our soul. It's an opportunity to see things in a kinder, gentler way.

SELF-AWARENESS

When you feel it is time to get to know yourself and you want peace in your life, there are some basic understandings that should come into your life. True happiness comes from inside us. It's not found by digging it up in the back yard. It doesn't grow on trees. It doesn't come from someone else. When we understand the difference between our personal inner happiness and outside events, we are on our way to understanding what happiness is.

If one day you receive a raise or a promotion to the head of your department, those are outside events. Something good happened that day and you might feel happy. When you find out the next day that the company is going out of business, you are sad. When we are happy inside of us for no reason at all, that is true happiness.

We need to understand that during our lives good and bad things will happen to us. If we can develop the ability to separate the outside world from the way we see and think about ourselves, we will be able to gain knowledge from each of our life's experiences. If something unpleasant happens, it may mean that it was time for us to move on in life and to grow in some way. Looking at events from that perspective, we can learn to calmly and happily accept life's challenges.

How we react to different challenges and problems can reveal our potential to develop our soul. Can we separate ourselves and our self-worth from the outside world? How do we feel about the current situation?

Again, it is how we decide to look at the particular situation. Our task on Earth is to develop our inner being to achieve the highest state of bliss inside our heart and mind regardless of outside situations. It doesn't matter what the outside world is doing around us. It is the way we feel inside and our joy of life itself that matters. The chart below shows how we can maintain our focus as good and bad things happen in our life.

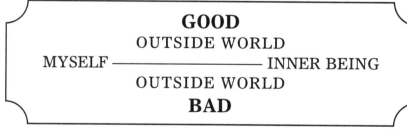

Viewing our life as an outside observer, we can be more objective to the lessons that life is bringing our way. Perhaps we don't understand the purpose of a lesson is until later. The important thing is to embrace every opportunity for your soul's development.

Let's say you are in a bad relationship, and it doesn't seem to be working out. You may make the decision to move on. Yes, it can be very painful at first, but as time goes on you learn the skill to love and forgive yourself for the mistakes that you have made. You become at peace within your own mind and body. All of a sudden, you are in love with your own life and just being alive. You don't need anyone else to make you happy because you have decided to enjoy life no matter what happens. Then, when you least expect it, someone appears out of the blue and a new relationship is started.

Take the knowledge gained from your previous relationships and apply it to the new relationship. You have learned from your previous experiences that this is an opportunity to continue your ability to interact with another partner. See the relationship as a separate entity that needs to be nurtured and kept strong.

In other words, what do you like about your partner? Why would you want to change them? Will your actions make the relationship stronger? Will it make the relationship weaker? Do you want a strong relationship? If your partner has some habits that you don't like, why was it okay at the beginning of the relationship but not now? Why would you want to change the very person that you fell in love with? Would you want them to change you? Realize that the relationship between the two of you is more important than being picky about minor things that don't matter much. Look at the big picture. No one is perfect, including you.

Develop the ability to overlook the small stuff, and work together to keep the relationship strong. This is an example of how we learn life's lessons as we begin to understand that there is no such person as a perfect individual. It's the ability to interact with other people that brings life's lessons to us.

The ability to seek and give forgiveness is the overall lesson. Be able to stay on the yellow brick road, and don't let the outside world take you off your path of personal growth. You are working on yourself and your ability to handle any situation with love.

Chapter 11
THE PLAN

HOW CAN I GET STARTED TO PLACE
MY EMPHASIS IN THE PROPER DIRECTION?

When you realize that everyone has a purpose in life, then you can begin the search for your purpose. You need to develop a plan that you can follow to develop your own soul and be true to yourself. Start by learning to become your best friend instead of being your worst enemy.

Life will have its ups and downs, but you will need to be true to yourself. Understand that every situation is a learning experience and an opportunity to develop your soul!

The situations you experience don't make you a certain type of person. The situations reveal what kind of person you are to that point in your development. You may be happy or unhappy with the way you responded to the situation.

However, when you look at the situation as a learning opportunity, it will show you the value of both your good and bad experiences. Each experience has a lesson for us. We can move forward with our spiritual growth if we participate with life.

Today I understand what my true responsibility is in

this lifetime. I now awaken the sleeping giant within me, and I will place my focus on the development of my soul! I will make my life plan knowing my true responsibility. The search for inner peace starts within me as I decide to change my thought patterns to become a kind, considerate person.

STARTING TO UNDERSTAND LIFE'S PUZZLE

Like a tree, we continue to grow from the time we are born until the time we die. As we mature our priorities change. It's important to understand that what is important today may not be as important in the future. Each phase of our life is very important to our development. How can we learn to run if we don't know how to walk?

When it comes to driving, you learn the routes to travel better when you are behind the wheel than if you rode with someone else. This is why we should embrace each opportunity to develop our soul. It may seem difficult at times.

The choices we make will determine if we move on to the next level of our development, or stay in the same old rut longer than necessary. The lesson will be repeated until we learn to accept it and understand that it's part of our development. Either way, it's a benefit for us because it's a learning experience.

If you know how to accomplish the task on the first try, or if it takes you a few times to understand it, what is the difference? Some lessons we learn faster than others! Life is not a race. So we can take time to understand what the purpose of the experience is and how it will help us in our development. Once we understand what life is all about, we can choose to accelerate our rate of development.

We do this by understanding that the key is how we think about each experience and how we react to it. The focus should be on our development and not the other circumstances involved with it. Our inner peace and happiness will come from within us rather than from the outside world.

Happiness is the way you decide to live your life. It isn't something someone else gives to you. When you are happy with life in general, you are much healthier because you send a positive message to your body. This is how we learn to become our best friend instead of our worst enemy.

Falling in love with your own life is the way to live life to the fullest. Look forward to the opportunity to learn about unconditional love each day. Starting with yourself, be like a child who looks at the world with wonderment and excitement.

Our thoughts are so powerful that they set the overriding tone of our attitude. Don't let your mind focus on destructive ideas. Concentrate on the good in the world. Release the bad thoughts that occur to you with unconditional love, and see the good in the situation.

For example, if someone is following your car very closely and flashing their headlights, trying to pass your car, you can look at this situation any way that you want. The driver could be someone who is a reckless driver, or it could be a husband who is trying to take his wife to the hospital because she is having a baby.

If you thought that some nut was on your bumper, it would probably make you angry. You would be upset.

If you choose to think someone is trying to get their wife to the hospital, you would gladly pull over, and you would feel very good about it.

The point is that the way you choose to view the same situation can have two completely different outcomes. How do you want to feel?

You have more power over you outlook on life and your feelings than you ever realized.

Do you want to become an angel on Earth and develop your soul to its fullest potential by seeing the best in each situation?

Do you want to create hell on Earth in your own mind by choosing to see the worst in each situation?

It's up to you through your power of choice! Developing our soul is our main purpose on Earth, and each experience has a lesson for us to learn.

TAKING CONTROL OF YOUR LIFE

How much time have you spent thinking about the way you want to live your life?

How much planning have you done to focus on the things you want out of life?

If this were the last day of your life, what do you think would be important to you?

Did you accomplish in this life what you came here to do?

WHAT DO YOU WANT OUT OF LIFE?

Wow! You had better think about this for a while! If you don't put thought into this what would happen? You would be drifting in the river of life going with the current of life forces without any direction or guidance.

WHAT IS THE PURPOSE OF YOUR LIFE?

Why are you here? What are you supposed to accomplish? How will you know when you are on the right path? Is there something more to life than what you have gotten out of life so far?

THE PURPOSE TO YOUR LIFE IS TO DEVELOP YOUR SOUL! THIS IS A RESPONSIBILITY THAT YOU CAN'T DELEGATE TO SOMEONE ELSE.

We have a tendency to want to fix everyone else except ourselves. With our eyes we see what is wrong with the world and everyone else. How can we develop our souls if we are looking in the wrong direction? The only person that we can control is ourselves. The only person that we are responsible for developing is ourselves. Our focus should be on ourselves and not someone else!

GROWING PAINS

How do you take control of your growth and direct it in the correct direction? One of our spiritual lessons is to learn to overcome our ego and follow our heart. When I say the word heart, I mean your gut feelings or intuition. Your mind is going to tell you to play it safe, but your heart is going to tell you to go for your dreams.

When we have the courage to go outside our comfort zone, we grow. The concepts of success or failure don't apply because regardless of the outcome, we are taking another step in our spiritual development. Even if our mind tells us that we have failed, we haven't really failed because we have worked on our spiritual development. We have gained a useful experience. It's like looking around a corner of a building. You can't see what is on the other side. There is a lesson for you in it either way.

How do you get in touch with your feelings? First, you need to understand that you are here to develop your own soul and that you are not here to change everyone else. The journey is within you and not outside of you. As you look at yourself through meditation, you will begin to understand what a beautiful human being you really are.

DEVELOP A MEDITATION ROUTINE

Take time the first thing every morning for about fifteen or twenty minutes to go into silence and meditate. Start out by making yourself comfortable. You can sit down, lie down or whatever position you choose, but make sure you are comfortable.

Close your eyes and take a deep breath. Then let your breath out slowly and relax. Repeat this process until you can feel yourself becoming completely relaxed. Do this in a manner that works for you, and repeat this process at least once every day.

I prefer complete silence when I meditate. If busy thoughts come into my mind while I am trying to meditate, I say to myself, "I release this intruding thought with love." It's almost like imagining that your mind is a bathtub full of water. When you meditate you are pulling the plug out and letting the water out. As the busy thoughts come into your mind, see them going down the drain as the water would, and release these thoughts with love. When the mental "tub" is empty, the thoughts will no longer come.

It may take a few weeks or months to master this meditation routine. Learning meditation is like going to school every day, if you stick with it you will learn. If you skip a meditation or school, you will miss the lesson for that day and lack the continuity you need to fit all the pieces together for the next lesson. If you aren't consistent, it will be like starting the lesson over.

The key is to meditate every day, and you will learn in a organized fashion. If you missed half of your algebra classes, how would you be able to do your algebra assignments?

Learning to meditate is not a race. So be patient and work on yourself regularly. If you stick with it, peace will come. This journey starts within one's self as you must learn to love yourself first and unconditionally without any exception. Heal yourself first before you go to heal the whole world. See the log in your own eye before you see the speck in another person's eye.

This book is about developing a personal relationship with yourself. Become your best friend instead of your worst enemy. There are steps to take as we go through our life's learning process. We are like a plant that continues to grow from the time we are born until the time we die. Each experience has a lesson for us. If we don't understand it, we will repeat the lesson until we do understand it.

When we have learned a lesson, we move on to another lesson. Our purpose in life is to learn these lessons. What is the purpose to these lessons? The purpose is to learn to overcome our ego and follow our heart. Yes, it's not only about what we do, but how we do it. You can do it with a smile and "get to do it," or you can do it with a frown and "have to do it." If you do it with love and a smile, you will be on your way to enlightenment.

The purpose of life is to develop our character to become kind, loving souls. Developing your soul and taking personal responsibility for your actions reveals what kind of person you are. A situation doesn't make you a certain kind of person, a situation reveals what kind of person you are. This is the lesson: you can handle the situation any way you choose.

When we realize we are in the process of developing our own soul through these lessons, we will use our power of choice more wisely. Choose to love, not to hate. Choose to build, not to destroy. Choose to help make the situation better instead of making it worse. If you can't help make it better, at least make sure you don't make it worse. Then you will be sending the right message through your soul's feelings that you are choosing to ascend and to be kinder, rather than to descend and create hell on Earth through your choices.

You see, the choice is yours and yours alone as you decide how to live your life. The rewards you reap will be gained from the seeds that you planted.

We grow from the time we are born until the end of our life. Like a seed planted in the ground, we grow at our own rate. Keep the seed watered and in the correct environment, and it will grow in due time. How long will it take until it produces fruit? Patience is the key to allowing people to grow at their own rate. Just as everything in nature grows at its own rate, we each grow at our own rate.

You can't force the growth of anything in nature. Why don't we understand that people grow when they are ready for growth? The growth of our soul is determined by our comfort zone and the choices we make. You can become the light and become an example for others to follow, but insisting that they do it "your way or the highway" is incorrect. There are many ways to reach the same goal.

As small children we are pounded into conformity. I wonder how many times an infant is told "no" until the time he goes to school. Is it any wonder why they might be a little gun shy? These are the years that they are learning self-confidence. They look to us for love and approval. We should spend as much time as possible getting to know our children. They are closer to the source "God" than adults because they haven't been on Earth as long. Look into a small infant's eyes and you will see unconditional love. How long does it take to lose that look? How many times do parents have to scream?

When I was young, I was showed how to tie my shoes once. If I couldn't do it, I got a whack with the belt. That certainly got my attention, but I still couldn't tie my shoes any better. I think discipline like this hurts a child's feelings. This type of treatment will make them mean.

Do you remember your first day of school? Were you excited? Were you afraid to go? This was when I first noticed that everyone was different. The sixth graders looked like giants to me. I had no idea what school was about. I wanted to go out and play. Some of the kids were from the city and some were from the country. My freedom was lost because I had to sit in class and learn my ABC's. A caged tiger had a lot in common with me because I was restless. By the second grade, kids are being labeled. Some kids are gifted and some are not. All kids are gifted, but are we smart enough to figure out what are their special gifts?

When we come into this world, everyone has a special talent that no one else in the world has in the same way. Our challenge is to find it. The talent might not be one that can be measured by test scores. A person may be born with a gift for music, art or nature, but lack math skills. Our goal should be to make sure that they understand that people have different strengths and weaknesses. It shouldn't be an issue that makes kids feel bad about themselves. Some of them turn to drugs and drop out of school because of the pressure. Schools should be fun. Teach the basics, but forget the grading of people. Tests should be given only to find a person's strengths and weaknesses. We should work on the weaknesses, but it should be done in a way that doesn't demoralize the student. We should turn kids on to education and life.

TIME

There are twenty-four hours in each day. It is up to us to choose how we spend our time. Rich, poor or middle class, we all get twenty-four hours each day. It's what we do with every minute of our life that determines the satisfaction and quality of our lives.

How do you want to spend your time on Earth? Do you realize that you have the same amount of time every day as the richest man on Earth? How would our thoughts change if we knew how many days we had left to live? If we had only thirty days left to live, would we spend our time the same way as before? What would the richest person on Earth pay for an extra day when his time on Earth was up? How can we take each day for granted?

I say we should be the master of our time and use it wisely! What is important to you? Can you develop the art of falling in love with your own life and time on Earth?

BE HERE NOW

The expression "Be here now" means to focus your thoughts on this very second of your life. If you are at work, concentrate on your job and give 100% effort to your work. If you are driving home, pay attention and get home safely. When you get home, leave the work behind and focus on your life outside of work. Don't have your mind at work when your body is at home. Leave your problems from work where they belong. Don't let them interfere with your life at home.

After you arrive at home, concentrate on being at home with your family. Pay attention and don't take your family for granted. Focus on your loved ones and put down the newspaper. Listen to what your family is telling you with 100% of your attention.

If your son wants to tell you about the ball game coming up on Saturday, take the time to give him your undivided attention. Spend quality time with your family and truly get to know their hopes and dreams. How many parents don't even know their children?

In the song, "Cat's in the Cradle," the father sings about how his boy wanted him to spend time with him. The father was busy and had every intention of getting together with his son, but he didn't have time to do it "today." So they never spent much quality time together, and the son grew up without his dad's involvement.

As the dad got older, and after his son had grown up and gotten married, he decided that it was important to start spending more time with his son. Unfortunately, by that time, the son was too busy and didn't have much time for his dad. As the song goes, "My boy is just like me." It would be a shame if it happened to you!

If we make the effort to "be here now," we can experience a dramatic impact on our lives, and how well we really get to know and appreciate the people who are important to us. After we lose a loved one, we begin to understand how important every minute of our life is.

A person will really miss a lot if they fail to tune into the beauty of everyday life. Take time to feel the wind in your hair, hear the birds sing, and smell the flowers. Don't allow yourself to be in such a constant state of hurrying and blind ambition that you miss out on the opportunity to enjoy the fullness of life.

The following two poems dealing with love may help you focus on loving yourself, your life and your fellow human beings.

LOVE YOURSELF

If I can't love myself,
How can I love anyone else?
God doesn't make any junk.
He even loves the punk.
How could I do any less?
Why do you think life is a mess?
Everything is happening as it should.
I'd learn life's lessons, if I only could.
I would be happy every day.
I would learn life's lessons that way.

UNCONDITIONAL LOVE

What is unconditional love
That we seem to lack so much of?
Is it being a friend
To want to make him bend
When he's down for the count?
Will we stop to help him out,
Should we go out of our way
To help someone every day?
What would God want me to do?
What would I do if it happened to you?
Would I look the other way?
Could I expect someone to help me today?
You are my friend,
I will help you until the end!

—Mannie Billig

THE PLAN

We must organize our thoughts in such a way that we are using our power of choice wisely and taking control of our actions. We can use three guidelines to help us get headed in the right direction.

We should start working on our own development, which is internal and isn't affected by events or circumstances outside of our own body. We can accomplish this by applying these principles to our thoughts about ourself. In other words, when we work on developing ourselves, then that is where our thoughts and efforts will be concentrated. We learn to become an observer of the happenings going on around us, and we don't let the outside world take control of our development.

The old saying applies here when thinking about what other people think about us. "YOUR OPINION OF ME IS NONE OF MY BUSINESS. BUT, MY OPINION OF MYSELF IS PARAMOUNT."

In other words, a thousand different people can see the same thing a thousand different ways. Every one of them can be right from their perspective. That doesn't mean that it's right for me. It's their opinion, and they are entitled to it. Personal responsibility for our development can't be delegated to someone else.

We must come to terms with our own thoughts and actions because that is part of our development. We can work on being a kind, considerate person. Our heart will know if we had the best intentions or not, so what the other person thinks of us is none of our business. We shouldn't let it bother us.

What I am about to share with you can be as simple as it sounds, or as complicated as you want to make it. These principles apply to all things in life, but we should start by applying them to ourselves first.

The first principle is
"GIVE OUT UNCONDITIONAL LOVE."

This means to love yourself first unconditionally, no exceptions. If you made a mistake and didn't handle something right, realize that you can learn from it and do better next time. How would we learn if we didn't make mistakes? We can develop our soul by learning how to seek and give forgiveness. The ability to forgive is a big key to personal development. A person who understands the flow of life understands the natural law that what you give out is what you will receive.

If we want peace and harmony in our life, then we should become kind and considerate people. The journey starts with the ability to love yourself and to become your best friend. Would a good friend lift you up when you are sad? Would a good friend be kind to you? Would a good friend want you to be happy? How can we want to do any less for ourselves?

The second principle is
"GIVE UP THE ATTACHMENT TO LOVE."

Love is something that should be given with no thought of receiving love in return. "I'll love you if you do what I want you to" isn't unconditional love. If you give love with no thought of the outcome, it will help you develop your soul in the correct direction. It's like playing tennis. Giving love is like hitting a tennis ball over the net, and what the other person does with it is up to them. You have done your part. What the other person does is up to them.

If someone asks you for five dollars to buy gas to get home, you have a choice to make. Do I want to help this person or not? If I choose to help, I have another choice to make. I can go to the gas station with them and pay for their gas because they might use the money for something else.

Or I can give up the attachment to the money and give it to them with love, knowing that I have done my part by giving up the attachment. What they do with the money is up to them.

Love should be given without thought of the outcome. It's something that you get to do, it's not something that you have to do. If you follow your heart instead of your brain, it will be done with the right intention. It will lift your spirit and you will begin to understand that we are all connected. When you do it with unconditional love, you really do give up the attachment to love.

The third principle is
"GIVE UP JUDGMENT."

When you give up judgment, it becomes apparent the only person that you are responsible for is yourself. How can we judge another person without walking a mile in their shoes?

If a thousand people saw the same thing, they would have many different opinions as to what happened. And every one of them would be right from their viewpoint.

The other person may be wrong from my point of view, but what if the person needed to experience that situation to develop their soul? Would we want to deny them the opportunity to expand their knowledge?

Most religions follow their interpretation of the Golden Rule. They are similar to each other and are in line with God's natural law. In essence, what you give out to others you will receive for yourself.

CONSIDER THESE VARIATIONS
OF THE GOLDEN RULE:

CHRISTIANITY
Do unto others as you would have them do unto you, for this is the law of the prophets.

JUDAISM
What is hurtful to yourself do not to your fellow man. That is the whole of the torah and the remainder is but commentary.

ISLAM
Do unto all men as you would they should unto you, and reject for others what you would reject for yourself.

BUDDHISM
Hurt not others with that which pains yourself.

CONFUCIANISM
Do not unto others what you would not they should do to you.

HINDUISM
Treat others as thou wouldst thyself be treated. Do nothing to thy neighbor which here after thou wouldst not have thy neighbor do to thee.

It would be a wonderful world if everyone followed the Golden Rule. Most people have good intentions and try to do the right thing. However, sometimes we allow our ego to run wild. Intentions are one thing, but living in reality is where we spend every day of our lives.

How can we turn our intentions into the reality of our daily experiences? Can we give the other person the benefit of the doubt? Can we give them unconditional love? It's all within our power to choose to follow the Golden Rule.

Sometimes we learn much faster when we make mistakes because it will increase our wisdom. As we begin to take control of our thoughts, we will become excited with our understanding of the knowledge received. It's only natural to want to share the knowledge with everyone we meet. Each person has a path to follow. It should be understood that we may have to learn in our own way. What worked for you may or may not work for me. This is true for the people closest to us because we don't want them to make the same mistakes that we made.

I may be able to give directions to a certain location, but there may be several ways to get there that I have not considered. It helps to understand that when you give unconditional love without attachment, you can give your opinion and not judge what the other person does with the information. It is enough to give love and wish for the best for all concerned. As we grow at our own rate, it helps to understand that each person is growing at their own rate also.

If you planted a seed and wanted it to bloom, you would see that it will bloom in its own time. People are the same. They learn their life lessons and bloom in their own time. We can't push the rate of growth of someone else. People learn at their own rate and not at the rate we desire for them.

It helps to understand that this is also part of our lesson. We can watch someone grow without injecting our will into the situation. We can just smile and understand that life is happening as it should.

Do we have the desire to seek the knowledge to make the correct choices to improve our understanding of our own soul's growth? This is something that we must come to grips with if we are sincere and really want to start growing on our life's spiritual path.

How do we do it? We should have the desire to get started! We should make the choice to do it, if that is our desire. We can use this knowledge and apply it to our everyday life. What good is the knowledge if we don't use it? Let's start with the basics. There are twenty-four hours in a day, and each person gets an equal amount of time. We start with our first choice, how do I want to use my time? Do I want to drift in the river of life, or do I want to take control of my life by making a plan to get me headed in the right direction?

What would I do today if I could do anything that I wanted to do? How do I want to live my life? Life is like a puzzle, put the pieces together in the right way and everything starts to make sense. Most people have drifted in their life and haven't taken time to think about what they really want.

If being with your family in the evening is important, don't take a job or open a business that requires you to work nights. Start to set the guidelines for your life.

Try putting your plans into writing, breaking out the categories as you see them. For example:

Goal 1. Develop my soul to its full extent.
Goal 2. Take control of my life and not drift.
Goal 3. Manage my time so that I can do the important things I want to accomplish.
Goal 4. Focus on what is important to me.

Some of the categories will go together. For example, the goal DEVELOP MY SOUL would include become my best friend instead of my worst enemy. How will you become your best friend? Have the DESIRE to improve your relationship with yourself, obtain the KNOWLEDGE to find out how to do it. Then make the CHOICE to do it. If you don't want to do it, or lack the DESIRE to do it, you don't have to do it. It's your CHOICE.

At some time in our lives we will be ready to make that choice and start to become our best friend. How do you see yourself at this time? Are you your best friend?

Step one is to understand that our mind or thoughts are very powerful tools to help us be all we can be. We can be our best friend or our worst enemy. We can manage our very thoughts and take control of them, or we can allow them to run wild and put fear into our being.

We are what we think. If we think that today is the greatest day of our lives, it will be the greatest day. But if we think it will be the worst day, normally it will be a bad day. The secret is to see yourself enjoying every experience life has to offer you. When you have a good outlook, you feel better and you want to improve your overall harmony with life.

If a negative thought comes into my mind, I can look at it in a positive way. If I am stuck in a traffic jam, it may have slowed me down and kept me from being in an accident. What a boring life it would be if we didn't have the opportunity to experience every emotion that life has to offer. All we need to do is take control of our thoughts and release the negative thoughts with love.

When we decide to be at peace with our thoughts, we will be much happier and much healthier. If we constantly worry all the time, it takes a toll on our health because we are putting unnecessary stress on our body. An example of this would be the difference between being relaxed and comfortable, or being up tight and irritable. If you learn to meditate every morning, it will help put your day in order. The small things won't bother you as much, and you will be happier. If you continue this routine, you will be able to feel the difference.

If you had a meal that didn't agree with you, it would be your choice to eat the same meal again and feel lousy, or you could listen to the signals your body is sending and not repeat that mistake. Do you want to feel great? It really is up to us to decide how we live our lives.

YOUR SOUL ACCEPTED THE CHALLENGE

When I asked myself why people and circumstances are so different, the answer that came to me was that my soul had accepted the challenge of this lifetime. I had chosen the circumstances that would develop my soul. I picked my parents and my physical characteristics. These choices let me see life from a particular perspective. I chose to develop my soul from this starting point. Could I learn to ascend and become a loving, kind considerate person under some very difficult circumstances? When we understand that we chose our situation in this life, it makes more sense to me why we are all so different.

Each person has to overcome the obstacles that they have chosen to work with. Do we realize how special we each are? If you were given a difficult assignment and you completed it with love and compassion, wouldn't it be a great feeling? It just doesn't make sense any other way for me. I no longer see the grass as greener on the other side of the fence as I accept the challenges of this lifetime. I will give every effort until my last breath to accept my life's challenges with love. I will move through each lesson as quickly as possible so I can take full advantage of this lifetime to become the angel on Earth that I am trying to become.

With this new found knowledge, I am able to understand it's not that life is unfair. It's that we made choices to start our soul's development from different and sometimes difficult circumstances. This gives me great comfort as to the different situations we find ourselves in. Why would some people have more support than others? Because some of us need more support than others. Take the opportunity to seize the day and awaken the sleeping giant in you and go for it.

BRING PEACE INTO YOUR MIND AND BEING

I believe the connection to God is in silence. With all the noise we get each day from external sources such as the television, radio, work noise, and road noise, is it any wonder that we can become frazzled by the end of the day? We can become shell shocked without even realizing what is happening to our being. It's our choice to take control of our environment and bring the peace and tranquility into our lives that we are seeking.

The first step is to realize that you desire an improvement in the quality of your life. Once you make the decision to work on it, you will be headed in the right direction. Start by taking control.

For example, turn off the television, radio and other outside noises. Don't buy a house next to an interstate highway. Start to meditate every morning for fifteen or twenty minutes every day to put yourself in order. Work on bringing peace into your mind and being. Don't let small things upset you. If this was the last day of your life, how important would it be that you didn't get the raise or promotion that you wanted?

Be grateful for the things that you do have. Count your blessings. You may not have the new car that you wanted, but some people don't have a car and they seem to make it through life.

MEDITATION

Meditation is the key to begin the journey to find our life's purpose.

We are here because we chose to come to the Earth plane to continue the development of our soul. Each soul picks their particular situation in this lifetime. As a result of this, we can work on the particular traits that we want to improve. Each life is designed to allow the soul a myriad of choices for development. When we understand that we are responsible for our own soul's development, we can put more thought into the choices that we make.

Before we can heal the whole world, we are told to heal ourselves first. We have the choice to ascend and become angels on Earth through our power of choice, or we can create hell in our own mind's eye. It is up to each person to decide their own path.

When we realize that our very thoughts create our own reality, we can become wiser human beings. The journey to find ourself is within our hearts and not in the exterior world. The old saying, "No matter where you go, you have to take yourself with you," applies. The secrets of developing your soul and finding happiness lie within you rather than in the outside world. Once we know where to start looking, we can begin to find the peace and happiness that we are seeking.

True happiness isn't something that someone else can give to you. It is something that you give yourself. It's the way that you decide to live your life. We must learn to look at each situation as an experience to learn and develop our soul. It's an opportunity to see things in a kinder, gentler way.

The journey within starts with setting aside fifteen to twenty minutes to meditate each morning before you start your day. Approach it like a child going to school, and don't judge it. Make sure that you are comfortable and relaxed. You can sit in a chair, on the floor or lie down on your back, just make sure that you are comfortable and relaxed.

Close your eyes and relax your mind. At first your mind may have plenty of thoughts racing through it. Don't try to stop the thoughts. Just release them with love. Imagine that your mind with all its thoughts is like a bathtub full of water. Each thought is like water in the bathtub. Just as you would pull the plug on the bathtub and release the water, you will be releasing thoughts from your mind and letting them drift away without any emotional attachment.

As you meditate every day, the number of intruding thoughts will become fewer and fewer. Then a peace will come over you. This sense of peace will make you feel calm and relaxed. It's very important to meditate every day.

If you meditate on a hit-or-miss basis, you won't feel

the same effect that you will get if you dedicate yourself to doing it on a daily basis. After six months of faithful daily meditations, you will be much calmer and relaxed throughout the whole day. This will allow you to start your day with a good feeling that lasts the entire day.

I cannot over emphasize how important meditation is in your personal development. You should approach your meditation with heroic persistence. You will only get out of meditation what you put into it. The choice is yours. You can make the choice to improve the quality of your life. If not today, then when will you start?

You may have the same issues to deal with on a daily basis, but the way you look at them may change if you so choose. You may find that sometimes in life you might not get what you think you want. However, the way you feel about your disappointments may change if you choose to look at them differently. Maybe you didn't get what you wanted, but now you understand that something better is on the horizon for you!

Chapter 12
THE POWER OF CHOICE

In the summer of 1995, I went to Greenville, Pennsylvania for my thirty-fifth high school reunion. I went to see some friends who still lived in Greenville. As we got to talking about life in general, one of my friends was complaining about the overall state of the economy in northwestern Pennsylvania. This area once had many steel mills and plants that produced railroad cars. Most of the plants had either shut down or were scaled back. In addition, most of the downtown area was in decay and had plenty of vacancies.

My friend made a statement that has stuck with me through the years. He said, "When is the government going to do something about our situation?" The thoughts that ran through my mind were, "Why are you counting on the government to do something? When are you going to take responsibility for your own situation and life?"

When a problem arises, some people immediately look for someone to blame. Sometimes the solution to a problem depends on how you want to look at it. Do you want to feel that everything is out of your control and that you are a victim? Do you want to just stand by and watch what happens? Do you want to wonder what happened, or do you want to make it happen? I know it sounds very easy, but what is our alternative? Why should we spend our time and energy thinking about things beyond our control? Why not clear the cobwebs out of our mind and start to think about things we can do and control for ourselves?

Over the years I have read several articles in *Entrepreneur* magazine that helped me understand that America is the land of opportunity. For example, there was a story about a man who had been transferred to California in the early Sixties or Seventies. He was earning around $100,000 per year with his company. He bought a big house and had just settled in from his move. His new boss didn't like him and fired him after only six months on the new job. Even though he had earned $100,000 a year, this man had lived from paycheck to paycheck. He only had about $400 in the bank.

As he thought about his alternatives, he came to the conclusion that he wanted to make sure he was never in the same situation again. So he went to a hardware store and bought a bucket, a squeegee, cleaning rags, and window cleaner. He spent a total of around $40 and decided to go door to door cleaning windows for money.

Inside of two years, he had a window washing business that did over $200,000 a year. He had figured out a way to do something about his situation using the skills and talent that he had. Losing his former job had turned out to be one of the best things that had happened to him because it forced him out of his comfort zone. He thought about what he could do in his situation, and he took action to create a better future.

There are many stories of how successful we can be if we put our minds to it. The song "They're Coming to America" reminds me of how people who can't even speak English come to America and are very successful. They get a minimum wage job, learn the language and save their money. Next thing you know they open a fruit stand or convenience store. They work hard and save their money, sell the fruit stand and buy a hotel.

Sometimes we spend our time and effort thinking

about the reasons we can't succeed. For example, you could say I only have a high school diploma, so how could I be successful?

Dave Thomas, founder of the Wendy's hamburger chain, didn't even have a high school diploma until he was in his sixties. He used to say if something came up in his business that he didn't know how to do, he would hire someone who knew how to do it. Dave Thomas figured out a way to get the job done. He didn't need to know how to do everything himself.

Bill Gates, one of the richest men in America, quit college to work on starting his own computer business. If you feel like you don't have enough education, when will it be enough! The guy who quit high school feels like he should have gotten his high school diploma. Likewise, the person who got a high school diploma feels like they should have gotten a college degree. Guess what? The person who did get a four-year degree feels like they should have gotten their Master's degree. Yes, the person who has the Master's degree feels like they should have gotten a doctorate.

So does a person who did get a doctorate have it made, or did they get their doctorate in the wrong field? You see it never ends.

A good education never hurts anyone, but it's not a guarantee that you will be successful in life. Get a good education if you can, but if you can't or if your education is in the wrong field, don't let that discourage you. I see a lot of middle aged people who feel that going back to school will answer all their problems.

Make sure that it's what you want to do and that it's not hiding from the realities of life. Take the tools that God gave you and do the work that you love to do. Never degrade yourself again. Enjoy life as it was intended to be. Don't be afraid to expand you comfort zone. Use the mind, body and spirit that God gave you. What do you have to lose?

You came into this world with nothing, and you will be leaving it with nothing but your soul's development. We were sent to the Earth plane to create and learn from the circumstances of our life.

Put yourself in a position to take control of your life. Understand that it's up to you to decide what type of life you want to live. Make sure you consider the fact that times and people change as they grow.

How will you spend your own time on Earth? Your time on Earth is the most valuable thing you have to share. If you want to have less responsibility, you could go to work for someone else. If you want more control of your life and time, you could have your own business. Just make sure that you understand that things could change and be beyond your control.

If you have planned your life with plenty of thought, you will be happy either way. You will understand that change is a part of life. As we consider all these factors, we begin the quest to find our unique place in life. The first question is, "Are we dreamers or doers?" Are we afraid to let ourselves succeed? Can we expand our comfort zone? Are we afraid to get out there and dance while the world is watching?

How else are we going to learn? If an opportunity comes your way in life and it is something you feel very good about, will you have the guts to go for it? Here are two examples to illustrate both sides of the decision.

I think it would be too risky to try that now. I can always do it later. So I stay at my present job even though I don't enjoy it. My life's effort will be put into the job I have now. They have been fair with me, and I want to do what is right. They're paying me reasonable money. Although I don't have much left at the end of the month, I can make ends meet.

Time goes by and you have twenty-five years with the company. Your new boss doesn't like you, or the economy goes bad. Maybe another company takes over and decides to consolidate their operations. During your twenty-five years, you were made several promises by good people who intended to keep their word to you about your future with the company. The only problem is that they were affected by the takeover and are no longer with the company. What will happen to you?

I personally got the message when one of the corporate officers asked me how to pronounce my name. I knew from that very moment that what I had accomplished in the past didn't mean a thing. I would be starting over and having to prove my worth all over again.

Over 2,000 management people got their walking papers. I was lucky because I was promoted. But it showed me that I could be out tomorrow just because someone didn't like the way I did my job. As I seriously considered what I would do, I made the decision to go for my dream of owning my own business.

I concluded that if I were working for someone else, it would be like being at the baseball game and being a spectator in the stands. I wouldn't ever get a chance to bat. If I owned my own business, I would at least get a chance to bat. Yes, it's true that I might strike out and not be successful. But, I could live with that because at least I had my turn at bat. I could always get a job. My experience was something that no one could take away from me. So why not put it to work for myself.

These things happen in the real world. Even if you are lucky enough to work for really good people, things still happen. Sometimes things are out of your control, and there isn't a thing you can do about them. Unless you decide to take control of your life! Even if you are the president of a company, you can be replaced in a day or two. It's sad to see people give the best years of their life to a company, then the company doesn't need them anymore. What will you do if it happens to you? Make a plan so you will be okay either way.

THE POWER OF CHOICE

During a seminar I was doing in Central Florida, I talked about the power of choice, and how God has given us more power than He had given the angels. We have the power to choose to love or hate, to build or destroy, to help or hurt. It is up to us.

During our group discussion, a lady became very angry because no one had ever told her that she had the power to choose. It seems strange that a grown woman would not realize that she had choices in how she lived her life. One might think that she would have been taught this in grade school or at least in high school.

As I thought back to my early years, I can't remember the power of choice being covered, either. During the writing of this book, I have used several examples of how people's lives could be much happier if we developed the skills to make good choices. How many opportunities during a day do we get to use our power of choice? Can we develop the skill to make good choices to the level that we can bring joy everywhere we go?

A kind word of encouragement can lift someone's day. It makes us feel better at the same time. Life is all about the opportunity to seek and give forgiveness. Take inventory of yourself. Are you a kind person? If not, you can develop this ability if you so desire.

Do you do all things with love? Can you see God in everyone you meet? Are you an extension of God's unconditional love? Are you starting to meditate every day? Have you awakened to your higher self, and let it do the work to tune you into the correct channel of higher consciousness? Have you released all negatives from your mind and body using affirmations? What good does it do to worry about things we can't control? What kind of message does it send to our body? Doesn't worry affect our health by the way we think? It all starts from our very thoughts.

Each situation is an opportunity to grow. How much will we grow in this lifetime? It's up to us to see the good in every situation.

HOW THE CHOICES WE MAKE AFFECT OUR LIVES

Some decisions that we make very quickly can change our lives. I wonder how many people have had their entire life changed by acting irrationally in a moment of frustration. There have been many people killed because someone lost their temper. I hear almost weekly about some case of road rage.

A short time ago, a driver was upset because another driver sped in front of him and cut him off in traffic.

The driver followed the speeding man and signaled him to pull off the road. The speeder pulled off, and the two men began fighting. As a result of their fight, the speeding man was stabbed to death in front of his young daughter. This angry driver will spend the rest of his life paying for that decision. And the young girl will have to live with the horror of seeing her father murdered.

What could make someone so angry that he felt he had no other choice than to take someone's life? What if the murdered man was speeding because he was trying to get somewhere because of an emergency? How do we know that was not the case? Wouldn't we want to help someone if we knew they had an emergency? Was that man's sense of ego and pride worth spending every day of his life in prison?

This kind of lack of control over emotions can have long lasting effects on the quality of the rest of our lives. Let's look at both sides of the road rage incident.

First, consider the man who was killed. Did he have to pull over and confront the man that killed him? Was his one-second decision worth the fact that his family and loved ones will never see him again on this plane of existence?

How will the decision he made affect the quality of life for his family? What lasting effect will it have on his daughter because she watched her dad get murdered? Will she ever feel safe in a car going for a ride again? Do you think she will miss her father? How does his wife feel about the fact that she will never see her husband again because of a split second decision? How many nights will she cry because she misses him?

What if he had decided not to let things get out of control on the highway? Would it have been better for all concerned?

The man who had been cut off in traffic could have said to himself maybe that guy cut me off in traffic because he has an emergency. I will help him by getting out of his way. This would have changed the outcome of the situation because it's hard to fight with someone who doesn't want to fight. Would the incident have been avoided if cooler heads had prevailed? Did the man who stabbed the other man put himself into a situation in which the only way to protect himself was to use a knife?

Would he take a different action if he could have that one moment back to live over? The point is that sometimes the choices we make have an everlasting effect on our lives. Also, they can have a lasting effect on everyone around us, too. These two men might have been friends if they had met under different circumstances.

It's easy to say, "Well, maybe these two guys were a couple of nuts who got out of control. They got what they deserved." I don't think so. But I do think that they let the situation get out of control because they were not thinking about the consequences of their actions.

It's up to each one of us to develop our thought process to the point that we see the best in each situation. This way we won't make a decision that could affect the rest of our life in an adverse way. I have heard many stories of how people's thoughts change when they know the whole story.

The following story is an example of this. Several people were riding on a bus. One of the riders was a young girl who was crying loudly. She was with her father, and she seemed out of control. Why doesn't he make her stop some of the passengers said to each other? The uncontrollable crying persisted long enough that one of the passengers asked the father if he would make his young daughter stop crying.

The father also seemed very sad. There were tears coming down his cheeks. The father said, "I am sorry she is disturbing you. I guess she is sad because we buried her mother today."

Once the other passengers bus found out the situation, the crying didn't bother them as much anymore. Their hearts went out to the daughter and father as people realized what kind of pain they must be in.

What a difference a little understanding can make about the way we feel. The people on the bus went from being angry to being very supportive once they knew the facts. How can we develop our hearts to give people the benefit of the doubt without knowing the whole story?

One day I heard an argument begin between one of my employees and a customer. The customer was in a bad mood and made a derogatory remark to my employee. I asked the customer if I could talk to him for a moment away from the other customers and employee.

He agreed and we walked to the other side of the store. As we talked and I assured him that we valued him as a customer, his whole attitude changed. He apologized for his actions. He explained that he was upset because he had buried his brother the day before and he was on edge. He told me his brother was handicapped and lived with him. His wife didn't like the fact that the handicapped brother lived with them. He felt that he never did enough for his handicapped brother. I told him that he was being too hard on himself as he did what he could. What more could anyone ask?

He thanked me for my concern. He said the incident in the store was the straw that broke the camel's back. In other words, his frustration had built up from his ordeal with his brother and wife. This pent-up frustration had to be released, and we received the brunt of it. It was not intentional, but that's the way things happen sometimes. We became friends from this encounter, and he used to stop by from time to time just to visit me.

When I was a manager of a large department store, a lady came in one day and asked the people in the office is she could speak to the store manager in private. When I arrived, she told me that she wanted to have the office door closed. I explained it was a company policy to have someone else present if the office door was closed. I had no idea what she wanted, so we had a witness affirm that the door was closed per her instructions.

When we sat down in the office, she opened her purse and pulled out $850 in small bills. She handed them to me. "What is this money for?" I asked.

She said a few years ago they had ordered a refrigerator from our store, but later cancelled it and had received a refund. Somehow the paperwork didn't reflect the cancellation or refund, and the store delivered the refrigerator to her home anyway. Her husband kept the refrigerator and never paid for it.

It bothered her so much that she would take a few dollars out of her grocery money every week and hide it until she had enough money to pay for the refrigerator. She said what her husband did wasn't right, and she wanted to clear her conscience. I thanked her and took the money to the cashier who gave the woman a receipt.

You see people are basically good and want to do the right thing. On one occasion at a small store, I was walking by and the clerk and customer were in a conversation. The customer had not received her change from a purchase. The clerk rechecked the cash drawer. The drawer was in balance, proving that he had given her the change. The customer told me that she didn't get her change, and if she didn't have the money when she got home, her husband would kill her.

I believed that the lady didn't have the money, but I also believed the cashier. So, I gave the lady around $100 in cash because I believed that she would be in deep trouble if she didn't have the money when she got home. She thanked me and went on her way, but felt the cashier still had her money.

The lady called the next day. She had found the money in another compartment in her purse. She really felt bad and returned the money that day. She said it was wonderful that we gave her the money, when in fact it was in her purse the whole time. She said our act of kindness renewed her faith in mankind.

These stories show that the basic nature of humanity is good. We just need to work on our ability to communicate with each other and make choices that will improve the quality of our lives and those around us.

WHERE HAS OUR SMILE GONE?

In the movie "City Slickers," three men try to regain their zest for life. They wonder why they have lost their smiles. Why had they gotten so serious? What would it take to find themselves and their enjoyment of life?

They decide to spend time at a dude ranch. They had never been on a horse or worked with cattle. After a short time on a cattle drive, they all realized how hard ranch work is and how much they missed their homes and careers. They didn't know if they would ever get back home because of the dangers on the cattle drive.

They started to realize what a wonderful life they had compared to the other people on the cattle drive. The cattle drive and their search for happiness made them realize what a good life they had lived up to that point. It's like being upset because you don't have the right color shoes to go with your outfit, and then you see someone who doesn't have any feet!

It is important to put life in the proper perspective in our own minds and realize how small some of our problems are compared to other people's problems. Why would we choose to make a mountain out of a molehill?

We will be able to improve the quality of our own life as we learn to see the forest while we are working in the trees. We can choose to no longer let little problems become big ones in our mind's eye. In the movie, the three men on the cattle drive made it home. Each one of them had a new outlook on their lives. They had been awakened from their sadness and despair. They had decided to enjoy every minute of their life.

Chapter 13
HEALTH

Many books have been written about how to be a healthy individual, from eating right to getting enough exercise and the sleep that your body requires. One way to improve our health is to develop our mind and body to a point that we can feel the effect that each action has upon our being.

For example, if you went out last night to a bar and had too much to drink, the message from your mind and body would develop into what is called a hangover. You would probably feel terrible. More than likely, you would experience a terrible headache and feel bad. What message is your mind and body sending? It's probably saying, "I don't like this very much. Please don't do it again because it's not good for me."

The question is why would we repeat actions that give us a bad feeling? Can we learn to be in harmony with our very being?

Let's say you didn't get drunk last night, and instead you went to bed early. You got up early, went for a three-mile walk, and meditated for twenty minutes. Next, you took your shower, and as you were getting dressed the feeling came over you of how wonderful you felt. It was almost like you were super human, and there was no doubt about it, you were ready for whatever the day had in store for you.

When you feel good, life seems to flow in a way that keeps you healthy. Dr. Deepak Chopra says it's our very thoughts that we send to our body that improve our state of health. He wrote an article titled "Manifest Mind" that shows how your thoughts affect your health. He said, "Life is like a tree and its root is consciousness. Therefore, once you tend the root, the tree as a whole will be healthy."

I consider the root to be my mind, my very thoughts. What I think about will usually manifest itself in my life. I knew a woman who thought that she would get cancer sometime in her life. She was right. She passed away from cancer. The question is, did the fact that she put the thought in her mind that she would some day have cancer cause the cancer to appear?

I am not a doctor, but I know that having negative thoughts in our mind doesn't do us any good. At the very least it puts you into a negative mood.

We can change the negative thoughts to positive thoughts. In other words, think about what you want rather than thinking about what you don't want. Envision yourself as being healthy and happy, and you will have a better chance of being healthy and happy.

Your feelings will give you guidance as to what your mind and body says is good or bad for you. Your body will tell you if the food you eat agrees with you the same as it will tell you whether or not alcohol agrees with you.

Sometimes eating the wrong foods can make you feel as bad as if you had gotten drunk. If you eat too late in the evening, you may not feel right the next day. The key is to recognize what makes your body feel good and what makes it feel bad. Wouldn't you want to feel good?

Most people haven't developed the ability to recognize that how they feel physically can be a result of the way they've eaten, slept and/or exercised. The ability to discern the effects of our diet and lifestyle is there, but we have to get in tune with it.

We need to try to handle each situation in a way that

makes us feel good about the end result. For example, the road rage incident where two men pulled off the highway and got into a fight that ended with one of them being killed. The man who survived the road rage incident will probably spend the rest of his life in prison or even face the death penalty.

What if one of them would have developed their feelings to the point that they knew the other man had an emergency and that's why he was in such a hurry? For example, maybe he was speeding because his wife was having a baby, and he was just trying to meet her at the hospital. Or maybe his dad was dying and he was trying to get to the hospital to see him one last time. Wouldn't each and every one of us want to let the man have the right of way through the traffic and feel good about letting him through?

If either of these men had set aside his ego and let the other man pass, wouldn't both of their lives have been much better? Instead of being dead or spending the rest of their life in prison, they could have continued to have a normal life. Wouldn't that have made more sense?

It doesn't matter if there was a real emergency or not, the end result would have been better if both drivers could have shown the kind of courtesy that people usually show in an emergency. Wouldn't it be better to think that you are helping someone else and feel good about it, rather than to feel rage against the other person and wind up with a knot in your stomach and angry feelings or worse?

Instead of having your stomach tied up in knots and having a headache, you feel good because you helped someone out who may have had an emergency. The ultimate goal is to leave every situation feeling good about your participation and the way you developed your thoughts and feelings about it.

Following your feelings and heart in all that you do is a big key to developing your mind, body and spirit to their full potential. When we get drunk or eat something that doesn't agree with us, it's obvious that our body doesn't agree with our actions. The next step in health is to continue to work with our feelings about our very being.

Have you fallen in love with your very life? Do you hate yourself? What kind of a message would hating yourself send to your body? Wouldn't your body feel bad? Would it create a lot of internal stress in your life? How healthy would that be? What would happen if you decided to become your best friend?

What if you decided, "Yes, I will fall in love with my own life, mind, body, and spirit. I will forgive myself when I make a mistake and understand that it's just part of my soul's development."

Do you think you would live a happier life without stress? Would your mind, body and spirit be healthier if you started to enjoy your life? When you are happy, you make the people around you happy. When you are sad, it makes other people sad.

Dr. Deepak Chopra says that when you are happy, every cell in your body is happy, and you will be a healthier person. Why do some people look much older than they really are? Could it be in the connection between the mind and body? The very way we think?

Have you ever heard someone complain about everything? They complain that people are no good, that people will lie to you and steal from you. As a result of their negative thoughts, most of what they think will manifest itself in their lives.

I believe that mankind is basically good and wants to do the right thing. Although I have problems like everyone else, I am developing my thoughts to see the best in each situation. It's my opinion that you can find just as much good in each situation as you can find bad. What kind of a message do you want to send to your very being?

I used to attend a church where at first everyone welcomed you with open arms. As I got to know my fellow church members, I realized that some of them were mean and cruel. I couldn't understand how they could tear people apart when they needed help.

Yes, someone may be an alcoholic and have other

problems, but why wouldn't we try to help that individual? Why were they so hard on the pastor? Why would they talk behind his back and not support him? He had given over twenty years of his life to the church. It had grown from a small church to around 3,000 members under his guidance.

I didn't feel right at that church, so I left because my soul wasn't being developed properly in my opinion. I felt sad about it, but I had to move on. I looked at other churches, but I decided that I wouldn't join another church until I found a place that practiced what they preached.

As I continued to pray and meditate every day, my personal relationship with God developed the way that I thought it should. After some period of time, I realized that I was looking for something in that church that I hadn't found in me. Once I found it in me, I could see that being a member of that church was a big part of my spiritual development and life's lessons. It was just how I chose to think about it at that particular time.

If I hadn't moved on, would I have learned the lesson? Once I changed, the whole world around me changed. The church wasn't wrong. It was the way I was thinking about it that was wrong.

I made the decision to give unconditional love to everyone, including myself. I decided to become my best friend. I gave up the attachment to the unconditional love that I was giving out. Then I decided not to judge what anyone else was doing. It helped me develop my thoughts to the point where I felt good about every situation because I was in control of my thoughts.

The question I asked myself is, "Are you giving unconditional love to everyone in every situation?" It was easy to do because it was my decision and wasn't affected by the outside world. If I forgot, I would give myself unconditional love, and I would do better next time.

It really made me feel good about myself and everyone I came into contact with. I was tested with family and friends. Someone even told me that they hated me.

As I thought about what they said, I asked myself, "Now do you love everyone unconditionally or not?" The answer I got was, "Yes, I do!"

I told this individual I was sorry to hear that they felt that way about me, but I wanted to make sure that they understood that I didn't feel that way about them. It was something this individual had to work on in their life, and I didn't want to accept it as my problem. They could chose their own thoughts and make their own decisions, but so could I. I wished them well and didn't dwell on their feelings because it was something I couldn't control.

It's a fact that not everyone in life is going to agree with you on everything, but it's part of our soul's development to learn to accept this and make peace with it. Other people are like actors in a play bringing lessons for us to learn about love and forgiveness. How could I have bad feelings about someone who was helping me develop my soul?

THE "THANK YOUR BODY" EXERCISE

When was the last time that you thanked your body for the effort it has made on your behalf? Our body allows us to participate in our life's experiences while we are developing our very soul. We are spiritual beings having a human experience through the use of our body.

What are the messages that you are sending to your body? Have you developed the ability to listen to the messages your body is sending you? What is your personal relationship with your body? Does it know how much you appreciate every heartbeat?

Sometimes we tend to take our bodies for granted. Are you giving it the correct food, exercise and the healthy lifestyle that it needs? What do you think of your body? Do you understand that you chose your body to develop your soul in? Isn't it part of your soul's challenge to become a loving individual in the body type that you chose?

Is it time to tell your body how much you appreciate every effort it has made to help you? Like the song goes,

"How could anyone ever tell you that you are anything less than beautiful?"

TRY THIS EXERCISE DURING A MEDITATION

Close your eyes. Starting with your feet, tell your feet how much you love and appreciate every effort that they have made on your behalf. How when you were exhausted, they kept you upright and steadfast.

Next move up to your legs and knees. Tell your knees and legs how much you appreciate the ability to walk and run, as well as the ability to bend your knees to sit down and stand up.

Then move up to the mid-section of your body. Thank your organs and digestive system for the functions that they perform. Thank them for the ability to digest food and to take the nutrients from the food to supply the energy that your body needs to sustain life itself.

Move up to your chest and thank your heart and lungs for keeping you going. Thank them for the very air that we breathe and our heart's ability to move the blood throughout your veins and arteries. Move to your arms and hands. Thank them for the ability to pick up things, and the ability to lift, flex, move, and all the things we do with our arms and hands.

Next move up to the neck and head. Appreciate the ability to see, hear, reason, smell, taste, chew, and think. Like a fine-tuned machine, it all works together to keep us going.

When we put all of these things together, we can appreciate the ability to feel and the ability to love. When we thank our body and come into harmony with it, we will be much healthier. Our body will appreciate the fact that we recognize how important each part of our body is and how much we love it.

Chapter 14
THE KINGDOM WITHIN

I realized that something was missing in my life. How could I find the kingdom within? What would it take for me to have inner peace in my life? Was happiness something I could find for myself, or did I need material objects to make me happy? Could I be happy regardless of my financial picture? What would it take to be an enlightened human being?

I went to *Webster's Dictionary* to find the definitions of the "kingdom within," inner peace, happiness, and enlightenment. I found out that these phrases are connected and helped me on my journey to find my purpose in life.

Let's break down the meaning of each word and phrase as defined by *Webster's Dictionary*. Kingdom within—KINGDOM: a land ruled by a king; one of three great divisions of existence, as the animal, vegetable and mineral kingdom. WITHIN: inside, as "look within."

According to these definitions, to find our "kingdom within" we should look inside ourselves. This means that we are the only ones who can find the "kingdom within." How do we look inside ourself? Well, it helps to know that the kingdom within isn't in the outside world. It's inside ourself. So we don't need to spend a lot of time looking outside ourselves to find the kingdom within. The way to go within ourselves is through meditation and/or prayer.

The following poem helps to illustrate the value of prayer:

TIME TO PRAY
(or Meditate)

I got up quite early one morning,
And rushed right into the day.
I had so much to accomplish,
I took no time to pray.
The problems just tumbled about me
And heavier became every task,
"Why doesn't God help me?" I wondered.
He said, "Why didn't you ask?"
I saw naught of joy of beauty,
The day sped on gray and bleak.
I asked, "Why won't the Lord show me?"
He said, "But you didn't seek?"
I tried to come into God's presence.
I used all the keys at the lock.
God gently, lovingly chided,
"My child, why didn't you knock?"
I woke up quite early this morning
And paused before entering the day.
There was so much to accomplish,
I had to take time to pray!

—Anonymous

Knock and the door shall be opened, if we so desire. Prayer and/or meditation are the keys to open the door to the "kingdom within." If we are looking for something, it helps to know where to look. Now that we understand the power of prayer and meditation, we know how to access the kingdom within.

The meaning of "inner peace" according to *Webster's Dictionary* is: INNER—internal, pertaining to the mind or spirit, as in inner experience. PEACE—a state of tranquility, freedom from fear or worries. When we have inner peace, it means that inside our minds and spirits we are free from fear or worries. The question is how do we become free from fear and worries?

Knowing where to start is the key to finding the path to inner peace. This means that our mind will realize a state of tranquility, freedom from fear and worry when we find inner peace. The opportunity to find inner peace is within our own minds. Therefore, we need to work on ourselves.

How do we work on our own minds? I recommend the book *As a Man Thinketh* by James Allen. This book states, "As a man thinketh in his heart, so is he." A person is what they think they are. This means we should work on our very thought process. We must see the best in each situation.

One evening I went with a group of people to a restaurant to have a late night snack. We waited quite a long time for the waitress to come to our table and take our order. Some people in our group were starting to get angry because of the wait.

After she took our order, we had to wait for an excessive amount of time for her to bring our food and beverages. When she finally bought our order, some of it was wrong and had to be corrected. She never did return to ask if we wanted refills on our beverages or if the food was satisfactory. When she finally brought the bill and left it with us, someone put a nickel on the table as a tip.

A couple months before this incident, I had begun to work on my thought process. The thought went through my mind that if we left a nickel for a tip, what point would we be making? What if the waitress was giving poor service because her husband had left her that day? What if one of her parents was sick? How would I feel if I knew that she had found out that day she had cancer?

I decided that we should give her the benefit of the doubt. I asked my friends to leave a large tip because we wanted to send love and kindness to someone who at the very least was having a bad day. This way we could send the right message to ourselves and to her.

One of the women at our table put the dollar bills into the shape of a heart. I am sure this lifted the waitress's day. We all knew this was the right thing to do. We left the restaurant with a smile.

This is one example of how we can improve our thought processes. We can make the best of each situation, leave with a smile on our face, and feel good about what we have done. Not only did our actions send a message of love to our waitress, it put our thought processes in a positive mode. We can make a positive difference in every life we come into contact with including our own.

The meaning of enlightenment according to *Webster's Dictionary* is as follows: ENLIGHTEN—to inform, shed light upon the way of truth or knowledge; ENLIGHTENMENT—forming nouns from verbs, denoting a condition.

Therefore, enlightenment is the condition of having light shed upon the way of truth or knowledge. We have the ability to develop our soul to its full extent by becoming enlightened. The kingdom within is in our very being. The way to access the kingdom within is through prayer/meditation.

We can find inner peace by changing our thought patterns to create an environment in our mind that brings peace and tranquility to our being.

Happiness is the state of being happy or joyous. Its synonym is bliss or joy. Happiness is the way you decide to live your life. It's not something someone gives you.

Life will have its ups and downs, and this is part of the lessons we are here to learn. How we react to a lesson will determine our rate of growth. Most people don't understand the value of each moment of our lives. We all live in the past with regret or in the future with fear based on our previous experiences. When we decide to be happy as a way of life, then we are pointed in the right direction.

I'LL BE HAPPY TOMORROW

I'll be happy tomorrow,
Because today my life is full of sorrow.
What happened to my smile;
It seems I haven't seen it in a while.
What happened to my dreams;
I have forgotten them so it seems.
Should I be happy today?
It seems too risky that way.
When will I awaken
And stop all this faking?
Why do we worry?
We seem in such a hurry!
Should my life end this way
Or should I be happy today?
If I had but just one day to live,
How would I choose my time to give?
Why not be happy today,
You see there is no other way!

— Mannie Billig

It's best to live in the now. Appreciate every moment
of your life. Become your best friend and seize the day!

Chapter 15
AFFIRMATIONS

In the book *As a Man Thinketh*, written by James Allen in 1905, he points out that we are what we think. A quote from this book, "As a man thinketh in his heart so is he," not only embraces the whole of a man's being, but is so comprehensive as to reach out to every condition and circumstances of his life.

"A man literally is what he thinks, his character being the complete sum of all of his thoughts. As a plant springs from and could not be without the seed, so every act of a man springs from the hidden seeds of thought."

If we aren't getting what we want out of life, shouldn't we begin to work with our thought processes? What do we really want? Have you ever thought about it? Do you want to just drift in the river of life without any thought of life's very purpose?

We can guide our life with the management of our thoughts. Do we want to be the wise master of our thoughts or the victim of circumstances? It is up to us as we use our power of choice to decide our path. When will we awaken to the purpose to our life? How do we find it?

There is a connection between our thoughts and our feelings. Can we develop our feelings in such a way that our thoughts are a result of what we feel? If you feel good, wasn't it because you were thinking in a positive manner?

As we begin to focus our thoughts on what we love and cherish, we can start to focus our thoughts on what we want. One way to get into the habit of positive thinking every day is to say a few affirmations daily. It is the conscious repetition of the same idea on the same mind that brings the awakening of the soul in the form of demonstration and results.

GUIDELINES TO FOLLOW
FOR AFFIRMATION SUCCESS

To realize that every demonstration is the result of thinking.

To know that every time I think, I open a channel for expression.

To realize that constructive thinking is right imaging.

To know definitely what I want.

To think only that which I wish to manifest.

To remember that perfect thoughts produce perfect demonstrations.

To see myself in the desired condition.

To make the thought clear, distinct and vivid as a picture.

To make the thought a moving one—an active one.

To dramatize my demonstration.

To rehearse it mentally.

To remember it is the intelligent repetition of the same idea on the same mind that brings the awakening in the form of demonstration.

To remember that the power of the inner mind does the work.

To realize that the outer mind decides and the inner mind expresses—does the work.

To have faith in the "I am that I am."

To understand the law of demonstration.

To use the law in a very matter of fact way.

To have heroic persistence and perseverance in using it.

To live it always.

In other words, to believe that what you want is actually happening. See it as a clear picture in your mind's eye without doubt. Feel it with every fiber of your being. Know that what you think will manifest in your life. Remove the negative thoughts from your mind like a gardener pulling weeds from the garden.

Just as sure as you plant a flower in the soil, know that when you feed it, water it, and give it the proper sunshine, it will bloom. Your thoughts will also bloom.

The question is are we planting weeds with negative thoughts? Can we remove those weeds from our thought process? With our power of choice we can, if we want to. Do we understand how the laws of the universe work? What you give out will be what you get back. If you give out unconditional love, won't you receive unconditional love?

If you think about and give out hate, won't you receive hate? Do you know what you really want? Can you manage your thoughts in such a manner to think only about what you want? Why waste a second of your life with negative thoughts? Can we see our desired outcome happening in our life?

Do we understand just as we plant a flower and watch it grow in its own time, our thoughts grow in their own time. Our job is to look after them and keep them nourished with love, and they will bloom.

Never doubt for a second that your thoughts will come to life. Realize the outer mind decides what you want and the inner mind does the work. Never doubt it. Be persistent in your thoughts about it.

The following list of affirmations can help you develop your feelings so you produce the desired thoughts to bring forth the desired result in your life.

124

AFFIRMATIONS FOR ADJUSTMENT

There is only one power, all good and true, everywhere evenly present and instantly available.

All things work together for good.

For with God, all things are instantly possible.

Everything works perfectly, divinely, in my life and affairs, being governed by God, the principle of all law and order.

My life is open to change.

I declare the law and order of God made manifest instantly.

All is done instantly, because God is the only power and the only cause.

All things unfold evenly, easily, smoothly, in my life and affairs, in perfect sequence in divine law and order.

Love overcomes all things. Love never fails. Love is fulfilling of the law. Perfect love casts out fear.

Divine love in me is an irresistible power creating my good for me instantly and consistently.

God in me is my instant and everlasting help.

I am keen, vital, alert in the activity of God.

I am forever undisturbed.

I am an expression of God's unconditional love. I am love.

AFFIRMATIONS FOR HEALTH

I love life.

I am healthy and thank my body for every effort it makes.

I am an open channel through which the healing currents of life flow.

God's love flows through every fiber of my being.

I will see the best in each situation.

I will use my power of thought wisely.
I am in harmony with the universe.
I am my best friend.
I will follow my heart.
I am peaceful and calm.

AFFIRMATIONS FOR WEALTH

The universe will supply me with everything I need.
My supply is equal to the greatness of my thought.
I am in alignment with natural law as I reap what I sow.
I have everything I need.
All supply comes easily.
I am drawing prosperity in all areas of my life.

AFFIRMATIONS FOR CREATIVE POWERS

I have all the ability that I need.
I can see things in new ways.
My purpose is to create.
There is no such thing as failure.
I am an open channel for new ideas.
I will lead the way.

AFFIRMATIONS FOR ENLIGHTENMENT

I am in the divine flow of life.
I know the way.
I am the light.
Each experience is an opportunity to grow.
I understand my purpose in life is to use my power of choice wisely.
I choose to love and not to hate.
I choose to live and not to die.
I choose to love myself unconditionally.

I choose to love my fellow man as myself.

I love God with all my mind, body and spirit.

These are some of the affirmations that we can use to get us on the correct path. Remember, it is the intelligent repetition of the same idea on the same mind that brings the awakening in the form of results.

Do you think this will help you? It will only help you if you feel it will, and you make the conscious decision to begin to tend your thoughts like a gardener. Pull the weeds of negative thoughts by removing them with love as a gardener would remove the weeds from a garden.

No, we aren't perfect and our feelings and thoughts won't change overnight. Just as a long journey starts with one step at a time, we begin to manage our thoughts one at a time.

We must have heroic persistence and perseverance in using our feelings and thoughts to bring the desired effect or changes into our life. This starts us on our journey to be enlightened human beings and knowing the way to inner peace and happiness. In a short period of time you will be able to feel if you are on the yellow brick road to inner peace and happiness.

You may have a bad moment or a bad day, but if you have heroic persistence and perseverance, you will be able to get back on the yellow brick road. When you are having a bad moment or day, begin by focusing on the negative thought and work on turning it into a positive thought or affirmation. The fact that you can now turn a negative thought into a positive thought is a major step in your development.

For example, what if you are driving and the car in front of you is going slower than you want them to. Because you're trapped behind them, their slow rate of speed is slowing you down. This situation could make you angry.

However, farther down the road you notice that a police officer has someone pulled over for speeding. Seeing this driver getting a speeding ticket can make you realize that the slow driver in front of you may have actually saved you from getting a speeding ticket. Can you see the good in this situation?

Or another example could be that you applied for a promotion, but didn't get it. Wouldn't it make you feel better if you knew that you were in line for an even better promotion, or that the promotion you missed was not a good match for what you truly want to do? Many times we think situations are a negative, and then later we find out that what we thought was a negative turns out to bring something better into our lives.

This book is filled with examples of how as my thoughts changed, my life changed. It seemed as if the whole world changed, but in reality I changed. I had a new outlook on each situation and what I was to learn from each new experience in my life.

I now know that the opportunity to expand my comfort zone was connected to my thoughts. I no longer had to be right in every situation, and I became more open minded to other points of view. I didn't have to accept them for myself if I chose not to. If they work for other people, that is fine with me. We are each just trying to find our own way in this lifetime.

Chapter 16
SUMMARY

We could try to get away from our daily life by going into a cave and meditating for thirty years. This would seem like a way to come to grips with our own personal issues. It would get us away from the daily trials and tribulations of life. The choice is ours, either we can embrace our daily lives, or we can try to escape them by not participating with the issues presented for our personal development.

If we choose to welcome the opportunity to expand our way of looking at our lives, we can progress as we desire. In other words, we need to embrace life's lessons with the understanding that these lessons are really for our benefit.

How long will it take us to realize that our purpose in this life is for our soul's development? As the old saying goes, "Wherever you go, you have to take yourself with you." You can't hide from your life's purpose because a lesson will follow you until it is completed.

When will you become the wise master of your soul's development? The choice is up to you. Can you change your outlook to a positive outlook instead of a negative outlook? When you greet each opportunity with a positive outlook, it will help you in your development.

THE CUP THEORY

Imagine your spiritual development as starting out as an empty cup. As you go through life, your cup would become filled with your life's experiences. The contents of your cup would be the measure of your spiritual development.

As we start on our own personal spiritual development we need to learn to love ourself unconditionally. We do this by applying the principles of love to ourselves. The first principle is to love ourselves unconditionally. The second principle is to give up the attachment to the unconditional love that we give ourselves. The third principle is to give up judging ourselves.

When we have fully developed to the point that we can be our own best friend and love ourselves under any circumstance, then we would be 50% spiritually developed. In other words, our cup would be half full of spiritual development. We would continue to learn our life's lessons. Also, we will have developed the ability to embrace each lesson with a smile and a good feeling in our heart.

After we have attained the love of self and our cup is half full, we move on to the next step in our growth. The next step is to learn to love our fellow man as ourself. We do this by taking the same set of principles we applied to ourselves and applying them to other people.

The first principle is to give unconditional love to our fellow man. The second principle is to give up the attachment to the unconditional love. The third principle is to learn not to judge others. And the fourth principle is to follow the Golden Rule: Do unto others as you would have them do unto you.

When you can see a part of God in everyone you meet and you love everyone unconditionally, your cup will be 100% full. You will be fully developed spiritually. You will understand that everyone is growing on their own spiritual path. And you will have become the wise master of your soul's development.

The next step in your soul's development is to have so much love in your heart that you teach people by the example that you set with your behavior. The way you live your life will exemplify that your cup is overflowing with the love in your heart. In this way, you can become an angel on Earth and an example of God's unconditional love for mankind.

Like peeling the layers from an onion, we can become more aware of our spirituality as we gradually drop our defense mechanisms one layer at a time. If you want to improve the quality of your life and learn your life's lessons, you can if you have the desire to do so.

I have made an attempt to supply you with some of the knowledge to get you started. The rest is up to you. Will you have the heroic persistence to meditate each morning? Can you learn to love yourself? Can you learn to love your fellow man as yourself?

Will you be able to become one of God's angels on Earth by letting the love in your heart to overflow from your spiritual cup by the examples that you set? Not by what you say, but by what you do.

Do you want to overcome your ego and follow your heart? It's as simple as following the three basic steps in our journey.

THE THREE STEPS
There are three steps to our journey:

1.) Learn to love yourself unconditionally. Learn to become your best friend by using your power of choice wisely.

Give unconditional love. Choose to give unconditional love in every circumstance in your life. Start with yourself.

Give up the attachment to love. Choose to give up the attachment to the unconditional love. Love that is given out only when people do what you want is not unconditional love.

Do not judge. Choose to give up judgment for the unconditional love that you gave.

Overcome your ego and follow your heart.

2.) Learn to love your fellow person as you love yourself. Do this by applying the same principles that we applied to ourselves.

Give unconditional love.

Give up the attachment to the love.

Do not judge.

Do unto others as you would have them do unto you.

3.) Teach the principles you have learned by becoming an example of God's unconditional love through your actions. Become the light and know that you really are an extension of God's unconditional love.

THE TUNNEL VISION

In November 2003, I attended a seminar at the Blue Sky Yoga Center in DeLand, Florida. While I was in a deep group meditation, I was taken to another dimension. I had the feeling of being in a state of bliss. As I started to go into the direction of the beautiful white light, one of my high school friends, Wayne Richardson, came from the light to greet me. He had been one of my best friends from my early years. He had passed away in his twenties.

I had often thought of Wayne through the years. I loved him as though he was my brother. I missed him and was so happy to see him when he came to greet me. He took me by the hand and asked me to go back toward the light with him. I went without hesitation. I felt happy just to be with him. In a short period of time we came to a tunnel. I could see that the light was coming from the other end of that tunnel.

Wayne looked at me and smiled as he took me into the tunnel. I could feel this strong feeling of love coming from the other end of the tunnel. As we started to get to the other end, I could hear a loud crowd roaring like I was at a football game in a large stadium. It reminded me of the times I played high school football, and the crowd would roar as we ran onto the field. Wayne led me out of the tunnel onto the field. The cheering of the crowd was wonderful. It was such a wonderful feeling that it brought tears to my eyes.

All of a sudden everyone from the stands rushed on to the field to congratulate me. I started to recognize everyone that I had come into contact with during my life. I wondered what was going on, and why was everyone so happy to see me?

Wayne told me that everyone was proud of the way I had overcome the obstacles in my life. "The lesson of life is to handle each experience with love," he said. I asked him if I had died during the trip to the light. He said I hadn't died. He said because I seemed to understand the purpose of life that I had been one of the ones chosen to tell humanity about unconditional love.

Wayne told me how everyone from the light is proud of each and every one of us. He further stated that life is a learning experience. As a parent would watch with pride as their baby learns to walk, the people from the light watch each and every one of us with great pride as we meet our lessons one by one. As a parent would help a baby when it falls while it is learning to walk, the people of the light support us 100% and are there to catch us when we fall.

We are never alone because they are watching over us. As I started to return from my trip to the light, a great feeling of love and understanding came over me. Life is to be lived with no regrets for the past and no worry for the future. We can all know that we have all the time we need to accomplish this part of our journey.

TO LIFE

Today is the first day of the rest of my life.
Today I start the journey to finding myself,
The person in me that I know is there.
I will live day to day with no guilt for the past
And not worry for the future.
I will live each day to the fullest.
Each day will be a new day,
No tomorrows, no yesterdays.
I will be the me I want to be.
I will accept the people in my life for what
They are, and not try to change them.
Life and people are ever-changing and
Intertwining. Everyone has their own goals
And purpose in this life.
My goals and purpose will be this:
To accept and love myself first,
For without that, my ability to love
Someone else is nonexistent.
When you have love for yourself,
the whole world is a brighter place.
Life will have its ups and downs,
But the new me will handle them with
Confidence and control.
And that will come from within me.

No one can make me a better person.
Only I can do that.
I had put myself in the pit of life,
And I pulled myself out.
With words and wisdom from some wise
And compassionate people, the doors to that
Pit have opened.
I now see the Light of Life.
The light made me want to live again,
To love again, and to hope and dream again.
This world is a beautiful place,
And I'm glad to be alive!
From this day on, my life will be in capable hands—
My capable hands.
I have fallen in love with life again—
My life.

—Author unknown

APPENDIX

COMPLETE MIND AND BODY ALIGNMENT
WORKSHOP INSTRUCTIONS

Two people are needed to perform the Complete Mind and Body Alignment. One person will be the recipient of the complete mind and body alignment. The other person will be the facilitator who works with the person asking for the alignment. The facilitator will allow the energy from above to come through them and connect with the God center of the person receiving the alignment.

Once both people have agreed to participate in the complete mind and body alignment, the person receiving the alignment will sit in a chair. In addition to the person receiving the alignment and the facilitator, it is a good idea to have available two or more other people in the room to act as spotters to catch the person receiving the alignment as they go limp and slide out of the chair onto the floor once they enter a deep meditative trance.

It is preferable that the recipient of the alignment sit in a chair with no back or arms. However, if the chair has a back, the recipient will sit in the chair in such a manner that the back of the chair will be at either their left or right side, rather than behind their back. Having the back of the chair in this position is necessary because it will make it easier for the spotters to ease the recipient to the floor. With the back of the chair off to the side, the spotters will have access to the recipient's back and can support the back as they lower the recipient to the floor. If you don't have extra people to act as spotters, then the recipient can start the alignment by sitting on the floor in an upright position.

The alignment begins with the recipient sitting in a chair as described above or sitting upright on the floor. The facilitator will be at either the recipient's left or right side. The facilitator then places one of their palms in a cupped position on the forehead of the recipient. The facilitator cups the palm of their other hand on the back of the recipient's head in the lower part of the back of the head that has a "knob" on it. It doesn't matter which hand is in either position.

Then, the person who is receiving the alignment says a prayer asking for the complete mind and body alignment. They make it known that they want the alignment energy to come to them by asking for the alignment in their prayer. The facilitator then says a prayer asking that energy come through them to help the person that wants the alignment. The facilitator keeps the palms of their hands in the previously described position throughout the alignment.

If the facilitator's hands get tired, they may switch the position of their hands so that the hand that was on the forehead moves to the back of the head and vice versa. After the recipient and the facilitator say their prayers, they will both go into a deep meditative state. It is very important for the recipient to relax and become the observer. The recipient needs to allow the energy from the facilitator to flow through their body.

After about five to fifteen minutes, the recipient's body will relax, and they will become rather limp. At this point, their body will slump out of the chair and onto the floor. If there are spotters present, this is the time for them to help ease the person to the floor and move the chair out of the way.

If there are no spotters present, the recipient should already be sitting on the floor. At the point where the recipient's body relaxes and slumps, the facilitator will ease them into a position of lying on the floor. The recipient should be placed in a comfortable position. Throughout this alignment the facilitator keeps their hands in the previously described position.

The entire alignment process takes on average about one hour. If the facilitator is unable to last the entire length of the alignment, someone may step in and relieve them. This would be accomplished by the new facilitator saying a prayer, and then the first facilitator would remove one hand while the new facilitator would place their appropriate hand in the same position and repeat this with their other hand.

During the alignment it is important to have silence in the room. Normally, it is best to have at least twenty people, ten teams of two, conducting the alignment at the same time. Each person is different. Therefore, it is necessary to allow the alignment to happen at a pace that allows each person to receive what he or she needs.

The alignment process is quite interesting. Some examples of what has happened in the past include people crying or releasing built up stress in their body. Parts of their body start to move by themselves. Other people talk with angels or become very happy and have a big smile on their face. Some people experience nothing.

Be sure to allow at least one hour for the alignment to work. The person receiving the alignment will wake up on their own when the alignment is complete. After they awaken and sit up, the facilitator places their hands on the top of the recipients head starting at the recipients forehead and moving their hands in a hand-over-hand motion from the forehead back to the "knob" on the back of the head. Start with both hands on top of the head side by side, then lift the front hand and put it behind the lower hand. Then lift the hand that was the lower hand and move it behind the other hand until you have reached the "knob."

When this is completed, hold your hand with the thumb touching the top of the head and the remaining fingers extended to the sky. Once you have completed the closing of the alignment, both the recipient and the facilitator say a prayer thanking God for the alignment.

Once the alignment and prayer are completed, the recipient and the facilitator can then switch roles, and the facilitator will become the recipient of an alignment from the recipient. The entire process is repeated.

After the complete mind and body alignment is completed on everyone present, everyone sits in a circle and there is a discussion of what was experienced during the alignment. The person receiving the alignment is given the opportunity to speak. The facilitator is also given the opportunity to speak. This is continued until each person present has described what they experienced both as a recipient and as a facilitator.

It is sometimes a wise idea to have people who don't know each other to be partners for the alignment. If friends or spouses work together on the alignment, there may be a tendency to hold back emotions that need to be released.

Anyone can do the complete mind and body alignment as the God force does the alignment, not the instructor. Don't get carried away by the ceremony. Just have good intentions and do the best you can. Effects of the alignment can continue for quite a while after the workshop. So it is not unusual for recipients to continue to feel effects of the alignment for two weeks.

MY ROAD MAP TO INNER PEACE

What do I want out of life?

Steps I will take to learn
to love myself unconditionally.

What do I want to change?

How will I make this change?

Ways I will use my time more wisely.

Steps I will take to learn to love others unconditionally.

MEDITATION NOTES

Important ideas that have come
to me during meditation.

ABOUT THE AUTHOR

Mannie Billig is a born philosopher and has always enjoyed helping people. In his book he uses examples of incidents from his own life to help others deal with difficulties in their lives.

In 1995, Mannie had his own spiritual awakening and dedicated the rest of his life to teaching people about unconditional love. He is a visionary who can see the good in mankind. He lives in Central Florida with his wife Judy.

Mannie Billig is available for lectures and seminars.

You may contact him at
www.manniebillig.com
or FAX: 386-860-5741

HOW TO FALL IN LOVE
WITH YOUR LIFE ON EARTH

ORDER FORM

Please mail the books ordered to this address:

Name_____

Address_____

City_____

State_____ Zip Code_____

Quantity_____ x $15.00 per book = $_____

Florida residents add 6.5% sales tax
or $.98 for each book ordered: $_____

Add $4.00 shipping and handling
for each book ordered $_____

Total amount enclosed: $_____

Please make check or money order payable to:

Richard Billig
P.O. Box 391313
Deltona, FL 32739

Prices and availability subject to change without notice.